MINTONS' ENAMELLED TILES.

The Tiles displayed in this book are, with the exception of those shewn on Sheet 16, which are printed patterns, and on the extra Sheet of Photographs, all Enamelled by a Patent process, known as "Reynolds's process," which was adopted in 1848 by the late Mr. Herbert Minton, and has ever since been carried on at MINTONS, (Limited), CHINA WORKS.

The process for the decoration of Tiles was early favoured by the late Mr. A. Welby Pugin, "the great restorer of Gothic Art," in the Houses of Parliament and in many other places, and the patterns in that style of ornament in this book are all from his hand.

Since the days of Pugin the use of these enamelled Tiles for decorative purposes has greatly increased, and there are now few houses without some examples either on the Walls, Grates, or Mantles, or inlaid in Furniture or formed into Jardinieres, but, perhaps, for no purpose are they more generally or more usefully employed than for Hearths, for which the body of the Tile is made of an extra strength; their cheerful appearance and the ease with which they are kept clean and bright, owing to their richly glazed surface, greatly recommending them for that purpose.

In some patterns the colors are on the glaze, but in all cases where the Tiles are exposed to much wear, such as for Hearths, &c., the Enamelling Colors are UNDER THE GLAZE, and therefore practically indistructible.

It should be understood that these Enamelled Tiles are not intended, and indeed are unsuitable for Flooring Tiles, which this Firm does not manufacture.

Mr. Reynolds, the patentee, who was awarded a medal of the 1st class at the Paris Exhibition of 1855, and also at Vienna in 1873, has had the management of the process at these Works since 1848, and although other manufacturers have lately adopted it, mostly in its simpler form, it is not too much to say that none have produced effects at all equal, for instance, to the Waverley and other series of monochrome pictures.

FOREWORD

I am delighted that Richard Dennis and Chris Blanchett have taken the initiative in presenting this beautiful reproduction of an original Minton China Works tile catalogue. The catalogue will become an indispensable acquisition for the tile enthusiast, collector and historian as well as the designer, who will find a plethora of inspiration within its pages.

Mintons diversity of output never ceases to amaze, from decorative wall tiles to encaustic floor tiles, from the classical to the naturalistic, Gothic to Japanese style, the tiles are depicted individually and as they would be seen in situ in borders, arrangements, floor layouts and fireplace panels and hearths.

The work of great Victorian designers associated with Minton, A. W. N. Pugin, father of the Gothic Revival, John Moyr Smith, and the radical art botanist Christopher Dresser come to life amongst its pages.

Tiles numbered 1327 and 1328 are taken from Pugin's 'Floriated Ornament' and Herbert Minton chose tile number 1084 for his retirement home at Torquay. Many examples in this catalogue including numbers 1065, 1110 and 1208 were exhibited in the tile courts at the international exhibitions of London and Paris in 1862 and 1867 respectively.

This is a catalogue that will be a constant source of inspiration and information to those who appreciate the beauty of Minton tiles.

Joan Jones
Royal Doulton Curator
(formerly Curator of the Minton Museum from 1977-1995)

INTRODUCTION

When Herbert Minton commenced full-scale production of 'encaustic' or inlaid tiles in about 1842, he needed a way of presenting his range to the public and also to distributors and architects throughout Britain and the Empire. As his representatives had to rely on horse or coach transport or occasionally on trains, they could only carry a very small number of samples on their journeys. The answer was to produce a printed catalogue with lithographed representations of the tiles. This was fine as long as the encaustic tiles were in two colours, but the introduction of majolica and printed tiles in the early 1850s meant that a new technique had to be found to reproduce these new polychrome products.

The answer lay with Chromolithography. This had been experimented with in the 1830s, but was a complex and expensive technique which involved producing a different stone for each colour. The colours then had to be printed from each stone in turn, exactly in register. Minton had been using a similar technique to decorate tiles since 1848 when Collins and Reynolds had patented their 'New Press' printing method so he was aware of the principles involved. He quickly saw the potential and by the early 1860s had produced his first 'full colour' catalogue.

With the rise in popularity of moulded tiles in the 1870s and 80s came a new problem. How did one capture the effect of the moulded surface? At first, tile companies had the designs etched or engraved, but this gave little indication of the depth of relief. Again the Minton Company was at the forefront of technology and introduced catalogues with photographically reproduced plates. The tiles were photographed as they came off the press or after biscuit firing; this gave the crispest image and alleviated the problem of reflection from the glaze.

The Minton Catalogue of c1885 reproduced here, represents the work of a number of top-flight printers: J. Fleming & Co of Leicester and Thomas Forman & Sons of Nottingham produced the chromolitho plates and M. Billing, Son & Co. of Birmingham reproduced the two photographic plates. This catalogue also has an extra sheet with pasted-on real sepia-tone photographs of some of the hand-painted tiles produced by the company.

The text pages at the beginning of this catalogue list the company's various series of Picture Tiles and will be of great value to tile collectors and historians, whilst the illustrations themselves will enable the attribution of many tiles in situ. We hope that the catalogue will also be an inspiration to modern tile designers, not to copy slavishly, but to show the possibilities available within the confines of a square or rectangular surface. Above all however, the catalogue stands as a supreme example of the printers' art!

Chris Blanchett

First published by
MINTONS (LIMITED), CHINA WORKS, STOKE-UPON-TRENT
c1885

Reprinted by
RICHARD DENNIS PUBLICATIONS, THE OLD CHAPEL, SHEPTON BEAUCHAMP, SOMERSET TA19 0LE
1996

ISBN 0 903685 50 7

LIST OF THE VARIOUS SERIES OF PICTURE TILES.

OLD TESTAMENT.

No. 1335. TILE 6 × 6. See Sheet 2.

A Adam and Eve driven out of Eden
B Death of Abel
C Lot's Wife
D Hagar and Ishmael
E Abraham Offering Isaac
F Jacob's Dream
G Joseph before Pharoah
H Death of the Firstborn
I Finding of Moses
J Samson slaying the Philistines
K Eli and Samuel
L David playing before Saul

NEW TESTAMENT.

No. 1346. TILE 6 × 6. See Sheet 2.

A Adoration of the Wise Men
B Going up to Jerusalem to the Feast
C Christ disputing with the Doctors
D „ Turning Water into Wine
E „ Stilling the Tempest
F „ Blessing Little Children
G „ Walking on the Sea
H Jairus' Daughter
I The Temptation
J The Crucifixion
K Christ Mocked by the Soldiers
L „ Appearing to Mary Magdalene

INDUSTRIAL.

No. 1342. TILE 6 × 6. See Sheet 2.

A	Smith	G	Barber
B	Painter	H	Weaver
C	Tailor	I	Shoemaker
D	Potter	J	Dyer
E	Tanner	K	Mason
F	Carpenter	L	Plumber

EARLY ENGLISH HISTORY.

No. 1344. TILE 6 × 6. See Sheet 2.

A Landing of the Romans
B Edy and Elgiva
C Lilla saving Edwin
D Galcactus
E Canute on the Sea Shore
F Boadicea
G Edward the Martyr
H Death of Harold
I St. Augustine
J Alfred and the Cakes
K Harold's Oath
L. Alfred in the Danish Camp

FABLES.

No. 1364. TILE 6 × 6. See Sheet 2.

A The Dog and the Shadow
B „ Fox and Goat in the Well
C „ Hare and Tortoise
D King Log and King Stork
E The Wolf and the Lamb
F „ Fox and the Crow
G „ Tortoise and the Eagle
H „ Fox and the Stork
I „ Lion and the Mouse
J „ Wolf and the Crane
K „ Monkey and the Cat
L „ Goat, Sheep, and the Calf in partnership with the Lion

FAIRY TALES.

No. 1366. TILE 6 × 6. See Sheet 2.

A Golden Locks	G The Little Tailor
B Snowdrop	H Jack and the Beanstalk
C Frog Prince	I Blue Beard
D The Sleeping Beauty	J Rumpelstilzchen
E The Six Swans	K Puss in Boots
F Cinderella	L Beauty and the Beast

FROM SHAKESPEARE.

No. 1408. TILE 6 × 6 See Sheet 2.

A	Romeo and Juilet	Act	I	Scene	I
B	„ „	„	III	„	II
C.	Macbeth	„	III	„	IV
D	„	„	V	„	VII
E	The Tempest	„	I	„	II
F	„ „	„	II	„	II
G	Cymbeline	„	II	„	II
H	Hamlet	„	I	„	I
I	Antony and Cleopatra ...	„	IV	„	IV
J	„ „	„	V	„	II
K	Winter's Tale	„	V	„	III
L	King Lear	„	I	„	I
M	„ „	„	V	„	III
N	Twelfth Night	„	II	„	III
O	„ „	„	III	„	IV
P	Midsummer Night's Dream	„	IV	„	I
Q	Troilus and Cressida ...	„	IV	„	II
R	Merchant of Venice ...	„	II	„	II
S	„ „	„	IV	„	I
T	Othello	„	I	„	III
U	Taming of the Shrew ...	„	IV	„	III
V	Much ado about Nothing ...	„	IV	„	II
W	Timon of Athens	„	III	„	VI
X	King Henry the IV ...	„	II	„	IV.

18 Selected subjects from this Series are also done tinted in Grey Monochrome. No. 1665. See Sheet 20.

Also in Sepia Monochrome. No. 1696. See Sheet 20.

SPIRIT OF FLOWERS.

No. 1347. TILE 6 × 6. See Sheet 2.

A	Waterlily	G	Foxglove
B	Lily of the Valley	H	Violet
C	Wild Rose	I	Anemone
D	Daisy	J	Primrose
E	Poppy	K	Snowdrop
F	Convolvolus	L	Lily

WATER NYMPHS.

No. 1409. TILE 6 × 6. See Sheet 2.

TWELVE SUBJECTS.

ELFINS.

No. 1410. TILE 6 × 6. See Sheet 2.

TWELVE SUBJECTS.

RUSTIC HUMOURS.

No. 1455. TILE 6 × 6. See Sheet 2.

TWELVE SUBJECTS.

From Tennyson's "Idylls of the King."

No. 1465. TILE 6 × 6. See Sheet 2.

This series differs from the preceding in having a background in another color.

A	The Lady of the Lake gives the sword to King Arthur	*The coming of Arthur*
B	Gareth entering the Town ...	*Gareth & Lynette*
C	Gareth and Lynette on their journey, Lynette jeers at Gareth	*Ditto*
D	Pelleas first sees Etarre ...	*Pelleas & Etarre*
E	Pelleas finds Gawin and Etarre asleep in the Pavillion	*Ditto*
F	Enid and Limours	*Enid*
G	Geraint slays Dorm	*Do.*
H	Elaine's body in the Barge	*Elaine*
I	Vivien puts forth the charm on Merlin	*Vivien*
J	Tristram and Isolt ...	...*The last Tournament*
K	King Arthur and Guinevere	*Guinevere*
L	King Arthur in the Barge with the three Queens	*Morte D'Arthur*

N.B.—This series is also done on Olive body. No. 1523. See Sheet 2.

Also in Browns on Buff, No. 1529, and as No. 1465, but with Buff in the Border, No. 1592.

The series is also done tinted in Sepia Monochrome. No. 1677. See Sheet 20.

"THE SEVEN AGES" IN BIRD LIFE.

No. 1653. TILE 6 × 6. See Sheet 18.

A	The Infant	E	The Justice
B	„ Scholar	F	„ Pantaloon
C	„ Lover	G	Second Childhood
D	„ Soldier		

No. 1654 is a foliage pattern to work alternately with No. 1653.

N.B.—Any of the foregoing Series 6in. Tiles may be done as 8in. Tiles by the addition of a Border all round.

FARM AND FIELD SUBJECTS.

No. 1422. See Sheet 6.

A	Cock	D	Duck
B	Hen	E	Rabbit
C	Turkey	F	Kingfisher

These subjects are in white, on a light blue (Turquoise) ground, and to work alternately with these are

Four Subjects of Field Flowers.

No. 1423. See Sheet 6.

Slightly done in the same light blue color, on white.

HUSBANDRY.

Twelve subjects in outline on 8 INCH TILES, arranged with leafage ornament as a border tile, to run either horizontally or upright.

This series is done in various coloring. See Sheet 2.

N.B.—This series is also done with a different border as a 6in. tile, No. 1727. See Sheet 18.

Classical Figures with Musical Instruments.

On TILES 8in. × 8in.

With background in Gold, No. 1466.
„ „ in color, No. 1501, on white body. See Sheet 2.
„ „ „ No. 1522, on buff body. See Sheet 2.
„ „ „ No. 1683, on celedon body.

A	Lute	E	Sistrum
B	Cymbals	F	Kithara
C	Harp	G	Tambourine
D	Double Flute	H	Pandean Pipes

Series of 12 Pictures from "WAVERLEY," tinted in Monochrome, from the original drawings by Moyr Smith.

On 8in. tiles in Grey Monochrome, No. 1607, and in Sepia Monochrome, No. 1697—see Sheet 20; also on 6in tiles, No. 1868. See Sheet 20.

A	Guy Mannering	G	Fortunes of Nigel
B	Kenilworth	H	Ivanhoe
C	Talisman	I	Old Mortality
D	Rob Roy	J	Antiquary
E	Bride of Lammermoor	K	Fair Maid of Perth
F	Heart of Mid Lothian	L	Quintin Durward

THOMSON'S SEASONS.

Twelve subjects from drawings by Moyr Smith.

On 6in. tiles, Sepia Monochrome, No. 1843. See sheet 20.
On 6in. tiles, Grey Monochrome, No. 1844. See sheet 20.
Or may be increased to 8in. by the addition of a border, in Sepia, No. 1875; in Grey, No. 1876.

A. SPRING: Emblematical.

"Come, gentle Spring, etherial mildness, come."

B. *Ploughing.*

"— Incumbent o'er the shining share
The ploughman leans, removes the obstructing clay,
Winds the whole work, and sidelong lays the glebe."

C. *The Rainbow.*

"He, wondering, views the bright enchantment bend
Delightful o'er the radiant fields, and runs
To catch the falling glory."

D. SUMMER: Emblematical.

"Child of the sun, refulgent Summer, comes."

E. *Celedon and Amelia.*

"Fear not, he said,
Sweet Innocence! thou stranger to offence
And inward storm."

F. *Musidora and Damon.*

"This cool retreat his Musidora sought,
* * * * *
And robed in loose array, she came to bathe
Her fervent limbs in the refreshing stream.'

G. AUTUMN: Emblematical.

"Crowned with the sickle and the wheaten sheaf."

H. *Reaping.*

"Each by the lass he loves,
To bear the rougher part, and mitigate,
By nameless gentle offices, her toil."

I. *Lavinia and Palemon.*

"He saw her charming, but he saw not half
The charms her downcast modesty concealed."

J. WINTER: Emblematical.

"See, Winter comes to rule the varied year,
Sullen and sad."

K. *The Snowstorm.*

"Now, shepherds, to your helpless charge be kind,
Baffle the raging year, and fill their pens
With food at will; lodge them below the storm."

L. *Skating.*

"And as they sweep
On sounding skates, a thousand different ways
In circling poise."

GASTRONOMICAL SERIES.

Twelve subjects, outlined and painted in colors by hand, on 6 × 6 Tiles, No. 1871. See Photo. on extra sheet. Also done on 8in. Tiles, by the addition of a border, No. 1880.

CATTLE SUBJECTS.

Four subjects, Cows, &c.; four subjects, Horses; four subjects, Sheep. No. 2017. On 6 × 6 tiles.

"ALBERT DURER" SERIES.

Twelve subjects, representing Medieval German Life. No. 2015. On 6 × 6 tiles.

SIGNS OF THE ZODIAC.

Quaintly represented by Twelve Figure Subjects, outlined and painted in colors by hand.

On tiles 6 × 6, No. 1762. See Photo. on extra sheet.

SHAKESPEARE'S SEVEN AGES OF MAN.

From drawings by H. S. Marks, R.A.

Seven subjects, outlined and painted in colors by hand, on 6in. tiles. There are two other subjects, Youth and Age, by the same Artist, treated in a similar manner, which may go with the Seven Ages if required.

On tiles 6 × 6, No. 1900. See photo. on extra sheet.

DAYS OF THE WEEK.

Humourously illustrated in 7 pictures (with an ornamental alternate tile) from drawings by Mrs. E. E. Houghton. These subjects are outlined and tinted by hand in light reds, and also in blues.

On tiles 6 × 6, No. 1759. See photo. on extra sheet.

OLD ENGLISH SPORTS AND GAMES.

Twelve pictures, sportively treated, outlined and painted in colors by hand.

On tiles 6 × 6, No. 1895. See photo. on extra sheet.

This series is also hand painted in Monochrome. No. 1896.

Subjects:—Hawking, Hunting, Fishing, Coursing, Shooting, Single Combat, Skating, Croquet, Chess Playing, Football, Cricket.

SCENES IN THE HUNTING FIELD.

Twelve subjects outlined and tinted in colors by hand.
On 6 × 6 tiles, No. 1898. See photo on extra sheet.
Also tinted in Monochrome, Blues or Browns. No. 1902.

FABLES.

Twelve subjects outlined and painted in Monochrome by hand in Blues. On 6in. tiles, No. 1897. See photo. on extra sheet.

NATURAL HISTORY.

Twelve subjects outlined and painted in Monochrome by hand in Blues. On 6in. tiles, No. 1899. See photo. on extra sheet.

VILLAGE LIFE.

Twelve subjects printed on 6 × 6 tiles, No. 1801. See sheet 16.

ANIMALS OF THE FARM.

Twelve subjects printed on 6 × 6 tiles, No. 1699. See sheet 16.

"WATTEAU" SUBJECTS.

Twelve printed pictures, on 6 × 6 tiles, No. 12. See sheet 16.

RUSTIC FIGURES.

Eight subjects printed on 6 × 6 tiles, No. 57. See sheet 16.

MINTONS LIMITED:—CHINA WORKS: STOKE-UPON-TRENT, AND 28, WALBROOK, LONDON.

EXTRA SHEET.

No. 1877. Panels 32 × 8.

Shaded Etchings: in deep Brown color, on Buff, Ivory, and Olive bodies, and in Blue on Ivory body.

No. 1762. Signs of the Zodiac. 6in. tiles.

12 Subjects. Painted in colors by hand.

No. 1895. Old English Sports and Games.

12 Subjects. Painted in colors by hand. Also in Monochrome: in Blue, No. 1896.

Postal Address—

MINTONS LIMITED,

CHINA WORKS,

STOKE-UPON-TRENT.

No. 1894. Heroes of Nursery Lore. Panels 24×6.

Tinted by hand in Monochrome: in Red or in Blue.

No. 1871. Gastronomical Series. 6in. tiles.

12 Subjects. Painted in colors by hand.

No. 1759. Days of the Week. 7 Subjects and

an alternate patt. Tinted in Monochrome—Red or Blue.

No. 1900. Shakespeare's 7 ages of man. 6in. tiles.

Painted in colors by hand. 7 Subjects. There are 2 other Subjects, Youth and Age, that may go with these. From drawings by H. S. Marks, R.A.

No. 1863. Panels 30 × 6.

Shaded Etchings: in deep Brown color, on Buff, Ivory & Olive bodies, and in Blue on Ivory body.

No. 1897. Fables. 12 Subjects.

Painted in Monochrome—Blue.

Tiles 6in. × 6in.

No. 1899. Natural History. 12 Subjects.

No. 1898. Scenes in the Hunting Field. 6in. tiles.

12 Subjects. Tinted in colors by hand, and also in Monochrome--in Blue or Brown, No. 1902.

Scale $1\frac{1}{2}$ inches to a foot.

MINTONS' (LIMITED) CHINA WORKS, STOKE-UPON-TRENT, AND 28, WALBROOK, LONDON.

EMBOSSED OR INDENTED TILES, IN RICH PERSIAN GLAZES.

THESE EMBOSSED TILES ARE PRODUCED IN A GREAT VARIETY OF COLOURED GLAZES, THE MOST USED BEING VENETIAN GREEN, BRONZE GREEN, TURQUOISE, OLD GOLD COLOUR, RICH BROWN, JADE, LIGHT YELLOW, CLARET, BLUES IN VARIOUS SHADES, &c.

Postal Address—
MINTONS' (Limited)
CHINA WORKS,
STOKE-UPON-TRENT.

Scale, 1 2 3 4 5 6 7 8 9 10 11 12 1½ *In. to a Foot.*
INCHES.

M. Billing, Son, and Co., Birmingham.

MINTONS' (LIMITED) CHINA WORKS, STOKE-UPON-TRENT, AND 28, WALBROOK, LONDON.

TILES, EMBOSSED OR INDENTED; ALSO WITH ROUGH, GRANULAR, AND PLAIN SURFACES, IN RICH PERSIAN GLAZES.

Postal Address—
MINTONS' (Limited)
CHINA WORKS,
STOKE-UPON-TRENT.

THE FOLLOWING SIZES ARE MADE WITH ROUGH, GRANULAR, AND PLAIN SURFACE:
6 × 6, 6 × 3, 3 × 3, 4 × 4, 4 × 2, 2×2, 4 × 1½, 1½ × 1½, 4 × 1, 1×1; also Plain only, 4 × ½ and ½ × ½;
also Diagonal Halves of the Square sizes, except ½ × ½.

Scale, 1 2 3 4 5 6 7 8 9 10 11 12 *1½ In. to a Foot.*
INCHES.

M. Billing, Son, and Co., Birmingham.

MINTONS (LIMITED)—CHINA WORKS: STOKE-UPON-TRENT, AND 28, WALBROOK, LONDON.

"MOROCCO" AND GLAZED TILES DECORATED WITH ENAMELS.

The patterns with an X added to the No. are made on an Extra Strong Body for Hearths, Fire-places, &c., but can also be made on the ordinary body for Walls, Dados, &c.

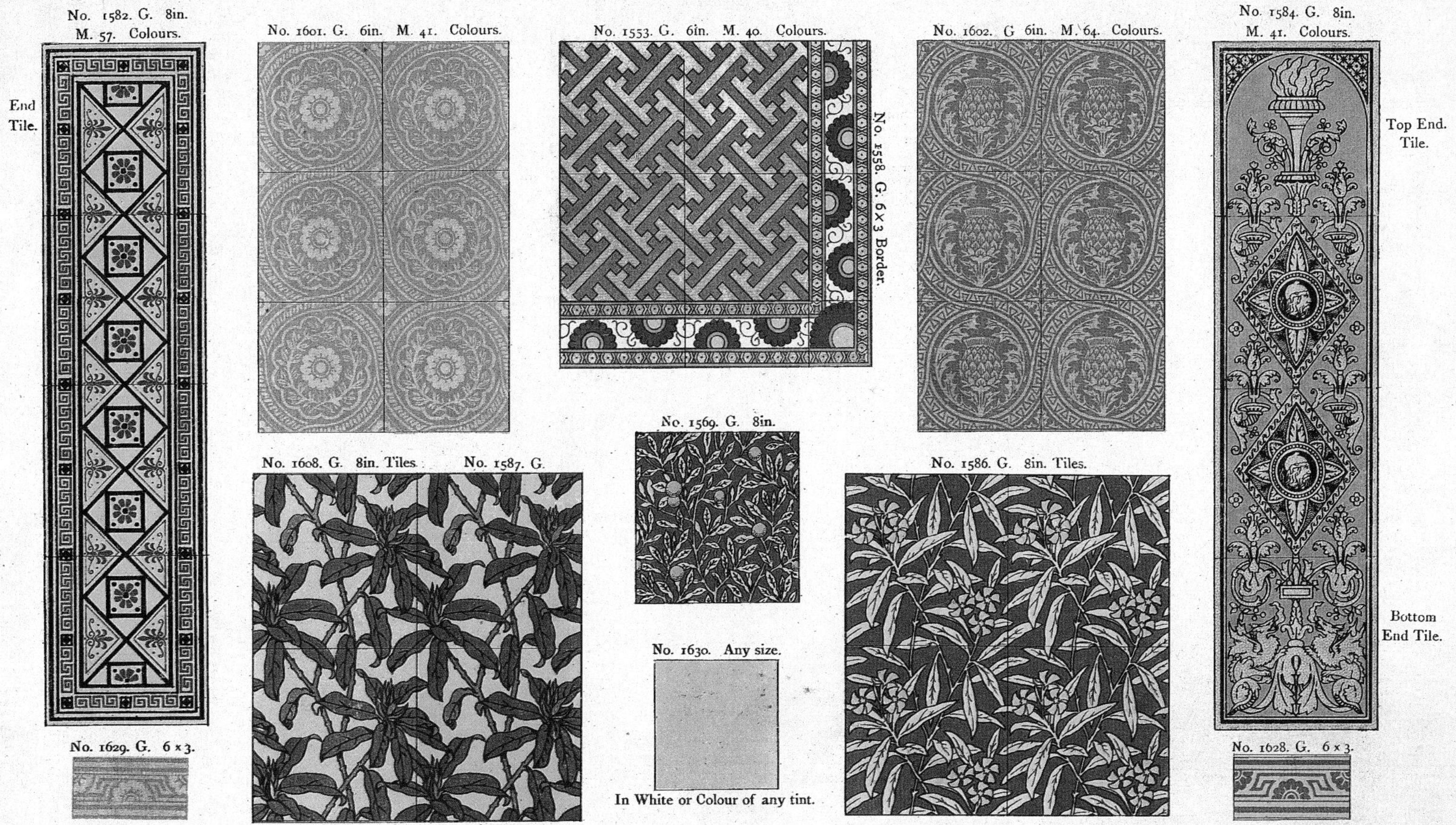

N,B—The above are patterns of the New Patent "MOROCCO" Tiles may be done in all tints of Colour. The surface being Granulated and Semi-Vitreous the Mat or Deadened effect is suitable for those purposes where Glazed Tiles are objectionable.

J. Fleming & Co. Lith., Leicester

Postal Address,—
MINTONS (LIMITED):—
CHINA WORKS,
STOKE-UPON-TRENT.

Scale 1 2 3 4 5 6 7 8 9 10 11 12 *1½ In. to a foot*
INCHES.

N. B.—Any of the "Morocco" Tile patterns shewn on the upper part of this sheet, may be done in nearly similar Colours with ordinary Glazed surfaces, and at the usual prices.

MINTONS (LIMITED)—CHINA WORKS: STOKE-UPON-TRENT, AND 28, WALBROOK, LONDON.

TILES RICHLY GLAZED AND DECORATED WITH ENAMELS,

FOR FIRE-PLACES, HEARTHS, FURNITURE, FRIEZES, WALLS, AND OTHER ARCHITECTURAL DECORATION, FLOWER-BOXES, &c.

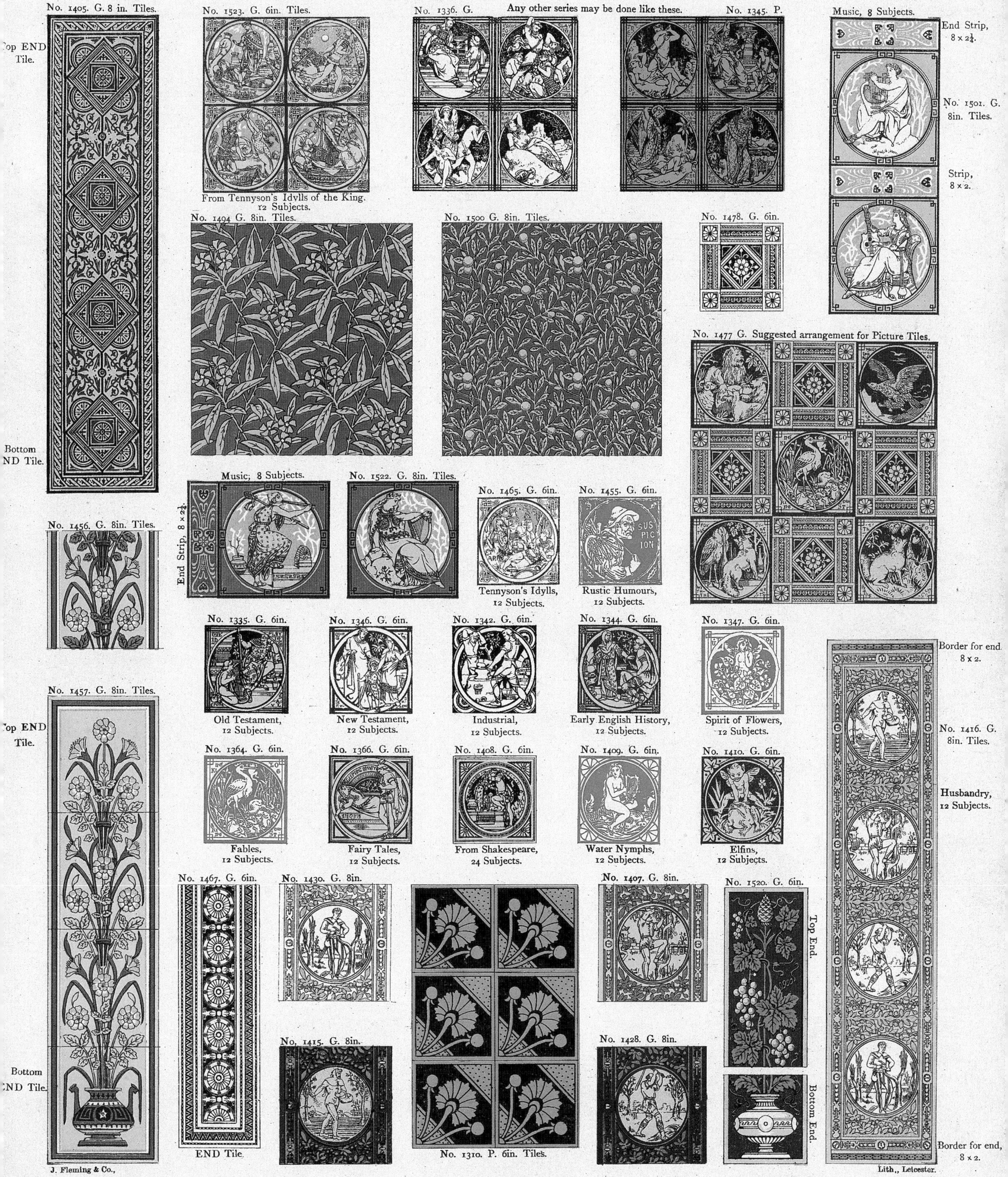

Postal Address,—
MINTONS (LIMITED):—
CHINA WORKS,
STOKE-UPON-TRENT

Scale 1 2 3 4 5 6 7 8 9 10 11 12 *1½ In to a foot.*
INCHES.

N.B.—Nos. 1416, 1407, 1428, 1430, 1415, are also made to run horizontally.

MINTONS (LIMITED)—CHINA WORKS: STOKE-UPON-TRENT, AND 28, WALBROOK, LONDON.

TILES RICHLY GLAZED AND DECORATED WITH ENAMELS.

These patterns with an X added to the No. are made on an Extra Strong Body for Hearths, Fire-places, &c., but can also be made on the ordinary Body for Walls, Dados, &c.

No. 1468. X. 6in. Tiles.

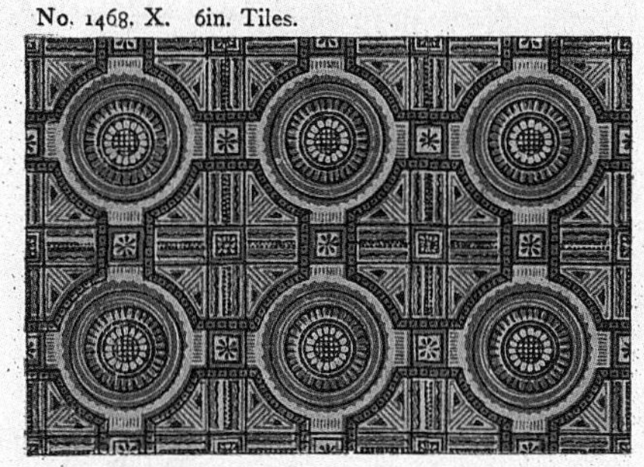

No. 1424. X. 6in. Tiles.

No. 1425. X. 6in. Tiles.

No. 1469. X. 6in. Tiles.

No. 1357. X. 6in. Tiles.

No. 1385. X. 6in. Tiles.

No. 1337. X. 6in. Tiles.

No. 1461. X. 6in. Tiles.

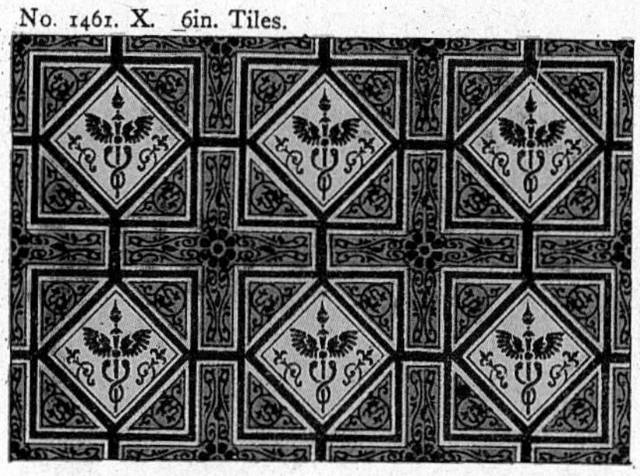

No. 1471. X. 4in. Tiles.

No. 1327. X. 6in. Tiles. No. 1328. X.

These two patterns will work either alternately or each by itself.

No. 1472. X. 4in. Tiles.

No. 1381. X. 6in. Tiles.

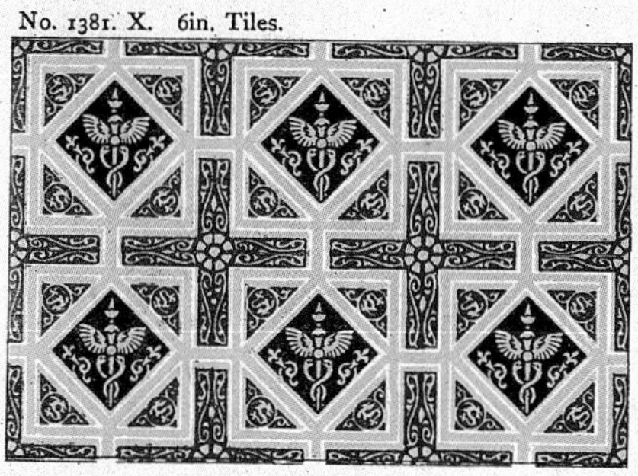

No. 1395. X. 6in. Tiles.

No. 1406. X. 6in. Tiles.

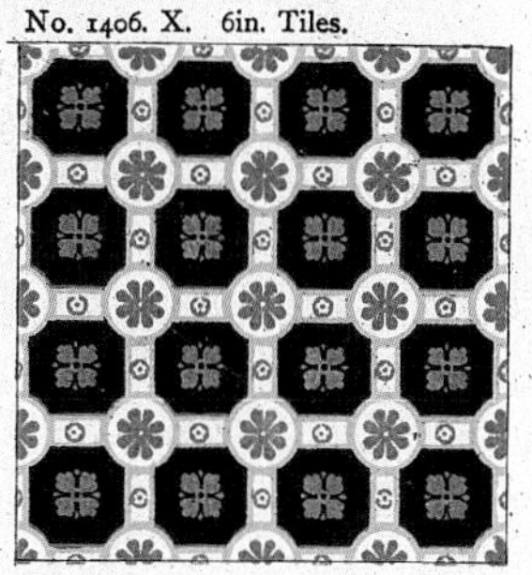

No. 1377. X. 6in. Tiles.

No. 1361. X. 4in. Tiles.

No. 1528. X. 4in. Tiles.

No. 1383. X. 6in. Tiles.

No. 1473. X. 6in. Tiles.

Postal Address,—
MINTONS (LIMITED):—
CHINA WORKS,
STOKE-UPON-TRENT.

Scale 1 2 3 4 5 6 7 8 9 10 11 12 *1½ In. to a foot*
INCHES.

J. Fleming & C. Lith., Leicester

N. B.—Four of any of the above 4in. patterns may be united in an 8in. Tile, but on ordinary body only, for Jambs, Sides of Fire-places, &c.

MINTONS, (LIMITED)—CHINA WORKS: STOKE-UPON-TRENT, AND 28, WALBROOK, LONDON.

TILES RICHLY GLAZED AND DECORATED WITH ENAMELS

These patterns with an X added to the No. are made on an Extra Strong body for Hearths, Fireplaces, &c., but can also be made on the ordinary body for Walls, Dados, &c.

No. 1118, X. 8in.

No. 1072, X. 6in. Tiles.

No. 1090, X. 6in.

No. 1096, X. 6in.

No. 1071, X. 6in. Tile

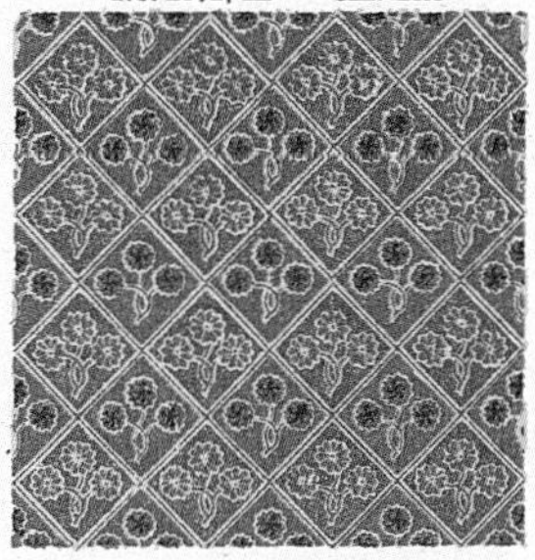

No. 1095, X. 8in.

1200, X. 6in. Tiles.

No. 1081, X. 6in. Tiles.

No. 1198, X. 6in. Tiles.

No. 1114, X. 8in. Tiles.

6in. Tiles. No. 1210, X.

6in. Tiles. No. 1292, X.

No. 1117, X. 8in. Tiles.

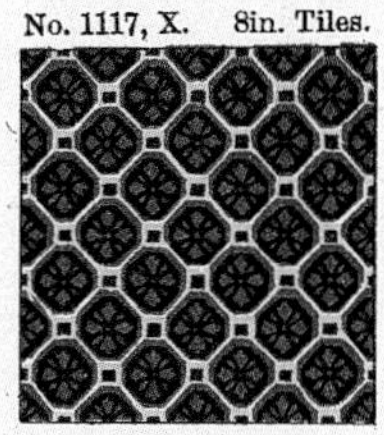

No. 1196, X. 4in. Tiles.

No. 1067, X.

6in. Tiles.

No. 1076, X.

No. 1112, X. 8in. Tiles.

No. 1107, X.

6in. Tiles.

No. 1159, X

No. 1066, X. 4in. Tiles.

No. 1070, X. 4in. Tiles.

No. 1089, X.

No. 1073, X.

No. 1082, X.

No. 1091, X.

No. 1103, X.

No. 1272, X. 4in. Tiles.

No. 1236, X. 8in. Tiles.

No. 1088, X.

No. 1085.

No. 1110, X.

No. 1145. 8in. Tiles.

No. 1237, X. 8in. Tiles.

6in. Tiles.

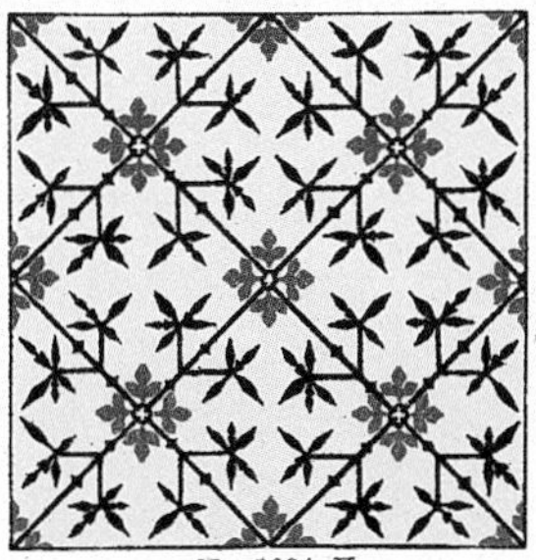

No. 1084, X.

6in. Tiles.

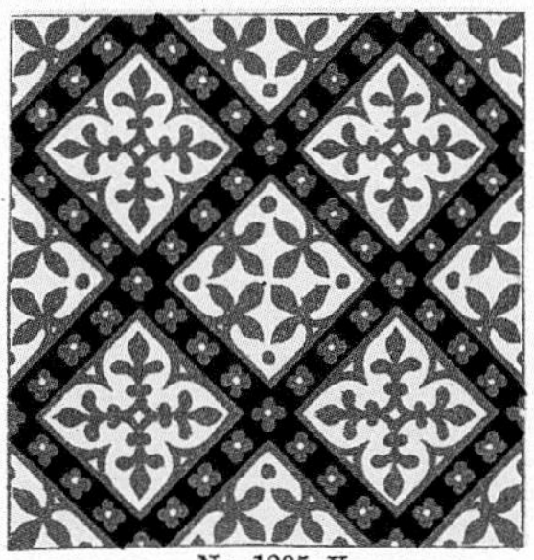

No. 1295, X.

6in. Tiles.

No. 1209, X.

No. 1298, X. 8in. Tiles.

Postal Address,—
MINTONS, (LIMITED)—
CHINA WORKS,
STOKE-UPON-TRENT.

Scale 1 2 3 4 5 6 7 8 9 10 11 12 1½ *In to a foot.* INCHES

N.B.—Any of above 8in. patterns may be divided in 4in. Tiles, which is a better size for Hearths, or four of the 4in. patterns may be united in an 8in. Tile for Jambs or sides of Fireplaces, &c.

T. Forman and Sons, Nottingham.

MINTONS, (LIMITED)—CHINA WORKS: STOKE-UPON-TRENT, AND 28, WALBROOK, LONDON.

TILES RICHLY GLAZED AND DECORATED WITH ENAMELS

These patterns with an X added to the No. are made on an Extra Strong body for Hearths, Fireplaces, &c., but can also be made on the ordinary body for Walls, Dados, &c.

No. 1206, X. 4in. Tiles.

No. 1283, X. 6in. Tiles.

No. 1221, X. 6in. Tiles.

No. 1270, X. 4in. Tiles.

No. 1228, X. 4in. Tiles.

No. 1240, X. 6in. Tiles.

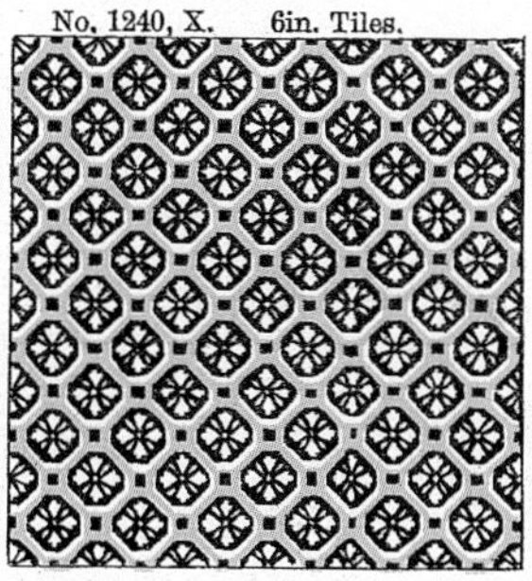

No. 1226, X. 6in. Tiles.

No. 1227, X. 4in. Tiles.

No. 1296, X. 4in Tiles.

No. 1304, X. 6in. Tiles.

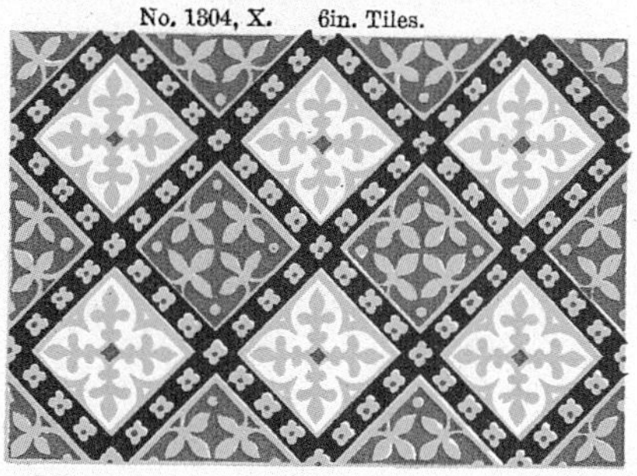

No. 1223, X. 6in. Tiles.

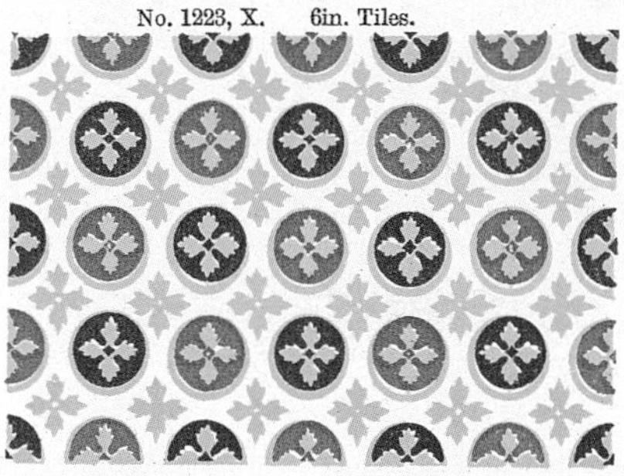

No. 1307, X. 6in. Tiles.

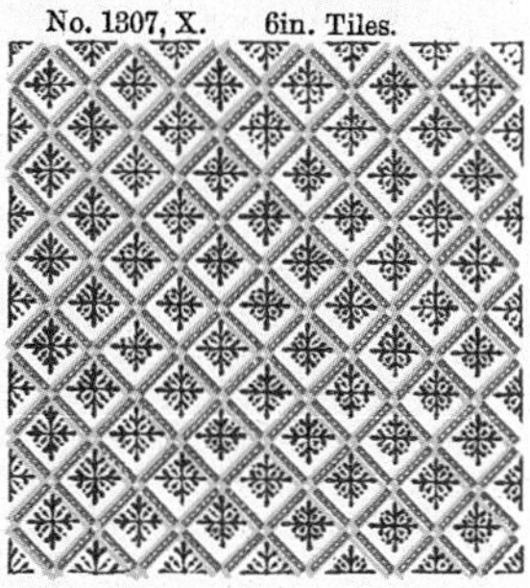

No. 1243, X. 6in. Tiles.

No. 1242, X. 6in. Tiles.

No. 1245, X. 6in. Tiles.

No. 1244, X. 6in. Tiles.

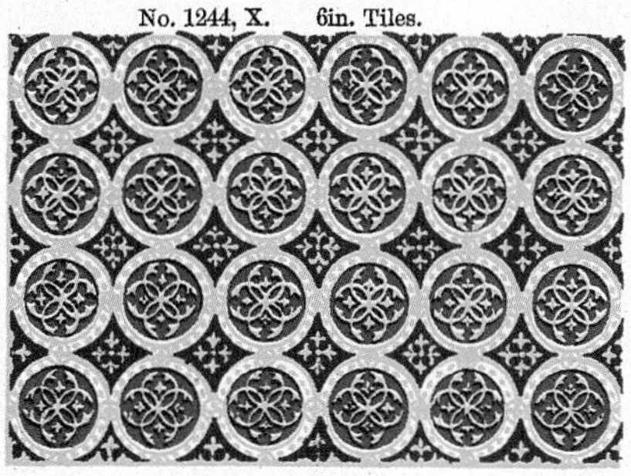

No. 1297, X. 6in. Tiles.

No. 1325, X. 6in. Tiles.

No. 1241, X. 6in. Tiles.

Postal Address,—

MINTONS, (LIMITED)—

CHINA WORKS,

STOKE-UPON-TRENT.

Scale 1 2 3 4 5 6 7 8 9 10 11 12 *1½ In to a foot.*

INCHES.

N.B.—Four of any of the above 4in. patterns may be united in an 8in. Tile, but on ordinary body only, for Jambs, Sides of Fire-places, &c.

T. Forman and Sons, Nottingham.

MINTONS:—CHINA WORKS: STOKE-UPON-TRENT, AND 28, WALBROOK, LONDON.

TILES RICHLY GLAZED AND DECORATED WITH ENAMELS,

FOR WALLS, FRIEZES, AND OTHER ARCHITECTURAL DECORATION, FURNITURE, FIRE-PLACES, HEARTHS, FLOWER-BOXES, &c.

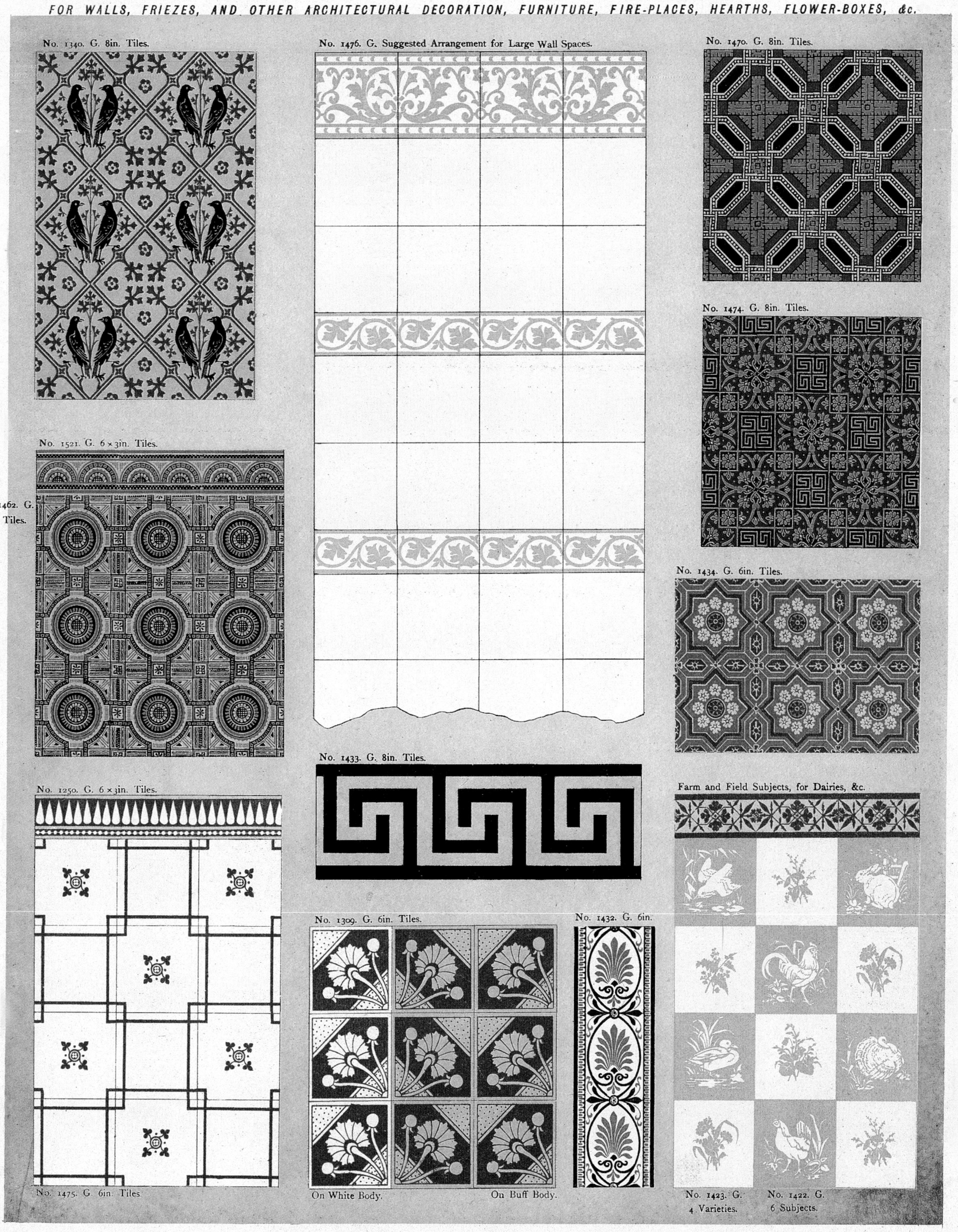

Postal Address,—
MINTONS:—
CHINA WORKS,
STOKE-UPON-TRENT

Scale 1 2 3 4 5 6 7 8 9 10 11 12 *1½ In to a foot.*
INCHES.

J. Fleming & Co., Lith., Leicester.

N.B.—Nos. 1470 & 1474, divided into 4in. Tiles, and 1434, 1462, & 1309 6in. Tiles, may also be done on the stronger body for Hearths.

MINTONS (LIMITED)—CHINA WORKS: STOKE-UPON-TRENT, AND 28, WALBROOK, LONDON.

TILES RICHLY GLAZED AND DECORATED WITH ENAMELS.

FOR FLOWER-BOXES, FRIEZES, WALLS AND OTHER ARCHITECTURAL DECORATION, FURNITURE, HEARTHS, FIRE-PLACES, &c.

No. 1401. G. 8in. Tiles.

No. 1397. G. 8in. Tiles.

No. 1459. G. 8in. Tiles.

No. 1415. B. 8in. Tiles.

Husbandry, 12 Subjects.

No. 1458 G. 8in. Tiles.

No. 1398 G. 8in. Tiles.

No. 1400. G. 8in. Tiles;— to be fixed diagonally.

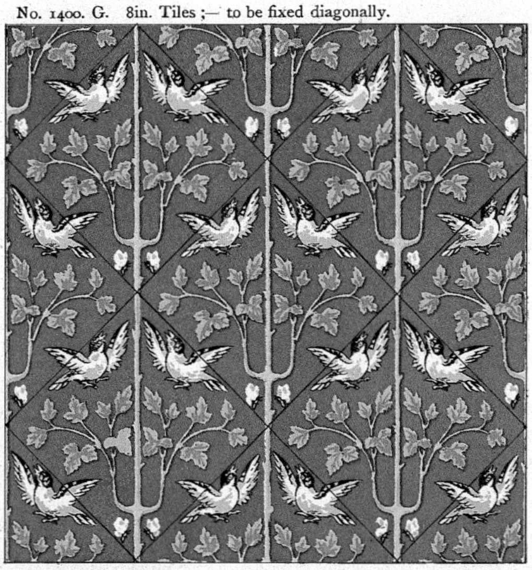

No. 1502. G. 6in. Tiles.

No. 1393. G. 6 × 3 Tiles.

No. 1464. P. 6in. Tiles.

No. 1495. G. 8in. Tiles.

No. 1419 G. 8in. Tiles.

No. 1460. G. 8in. Tiles.

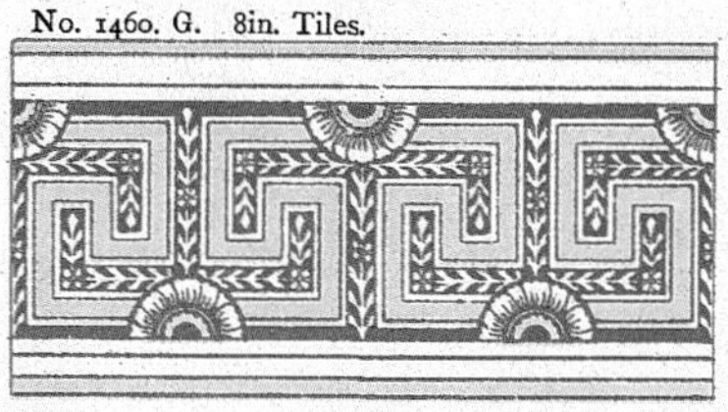

No. 1394. G. 6 × 3 Tiles.

No. 1378. G. 6in. Tiles.

Postal Address,—
MINTONS (LIMITED):—
CHINA WORKS,
STOKE-UPON-TRENT.

Scale 1 2 3 4 5 6 7 8 9 10 11 12 *1½ In. to a foot*
INCHES.

J. Fleming & Co. Lith., Leicester

N.B.—Nos. 1397 and 1398 are also made in 6in. Tiles. No. 1394 is also made as a Hearth Tile.

MINTONS, (LIMITED)—CHINA WORKS: STOKE-UPON-TRENT, AND 28, WALBROOK, LONDON.

TILES RICHLY GLAZED AND DECORATED WITH ENAMELS

FOR FLOWER-BOXES, FRIEZES, WALLS AND OTHER ARCHITECTURAL DECORATION, FURNITURE, HEARTHS, FIRE-PLACES, &c

No. 1302, A. No. 1302, B. No. 1302, A.

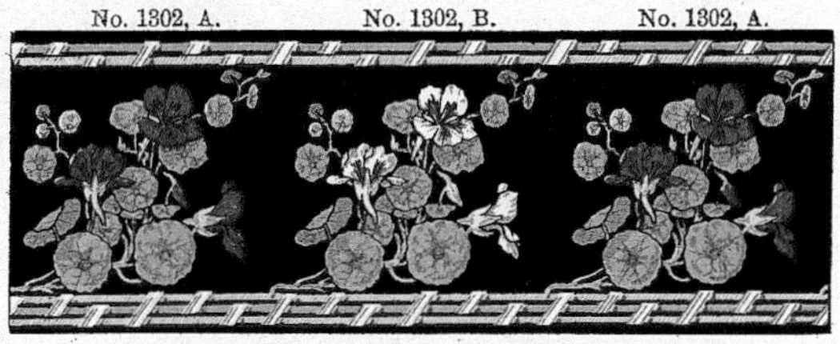

8in. Tiles.

No. 1303, G. 8in.

No. 1204, G, may work alternate with No. 1302, C.

8in. Tile.

No. 416, G. 8in. Tiles.

No. 1324, G. 8in. Tiles.

No. 1323, G. 8in. Tiles.

No. 801, G. 6in. Tiles.

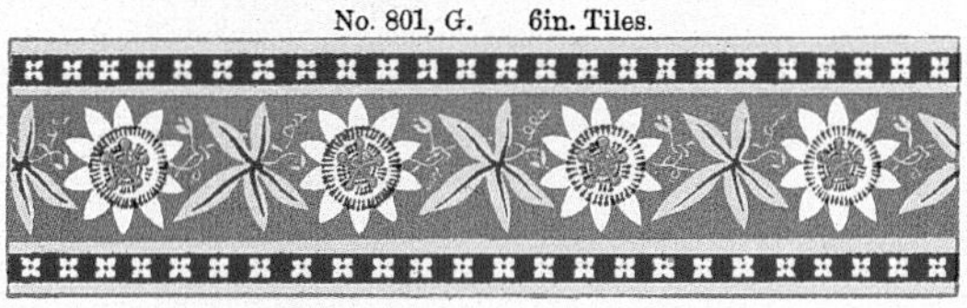

No. 950, G. 6in. Tiles.

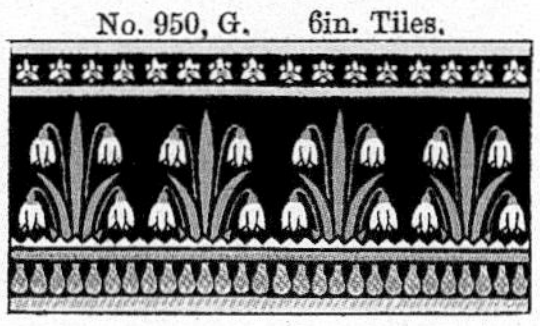

No. 968, G. 6in. Tiles.

No. 1022, G. 8in. Tiles.

No. 508, G. 8in. Tiles.

No. 402, G. 8in.

No. 986, G. 8in. Tiles.

No. 983, G. 7in. Tiles.

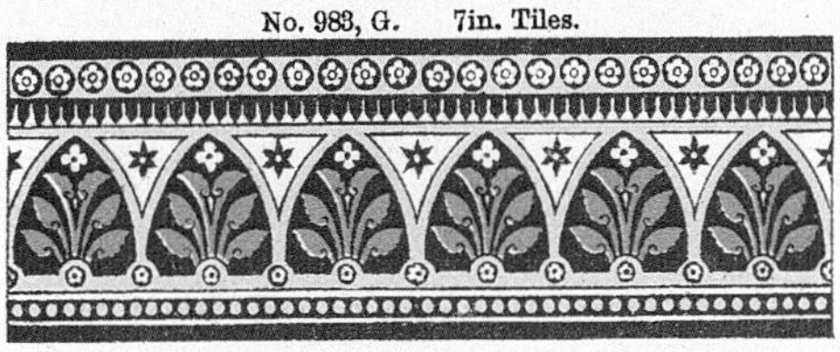

No. 1321, G. 8in. Tiles.

No, 995, G. 7in. Tiles.

No. 1143, G. 8in Tiles

No. 1208, G. 8in. Tiles.

No. 1148, G 8in. Tiles

No. 781, G. 6in. Tiles.

No. 574, G. 6in. Tiles.

No. 612, G. 6in. Tiles.

No. 1063, G. 8in. Tiles.

No. 848, G. 8in. Tiles.

No. 895, G. 8in. Tiles.

Postal Address,—

MINTONS, (LIMITED)—

CHINA WORKS,

STOKE-UPON-TRENT.

Scale 1 2 3 4 5 6 7 8 9 10 11 12 *1½ In. to a foot.*
INCHES

N.B.—Nos. 416, 1022 and 848 are also made in 6in. Tiles, and No. 950 in 8in.

T. Forman and Sons, Nottingham.

MINTONS, (LIMITED)—CHINA WORKS: STOKE-UPON-TRENT, AND 28, WALBROOK, LONDON.

TILES RICHLY GLAZED AND DECORATED WITH PERSIAN ENAMELS AND CHIEFLY OF PERSIAN DESIGN

FOR WALLS, FIREPLACES, AND OTHER ARCHITECTURAL DECORATION, FLOWER BOXES, &c.

No. 1190, P. 6in. Tiles.

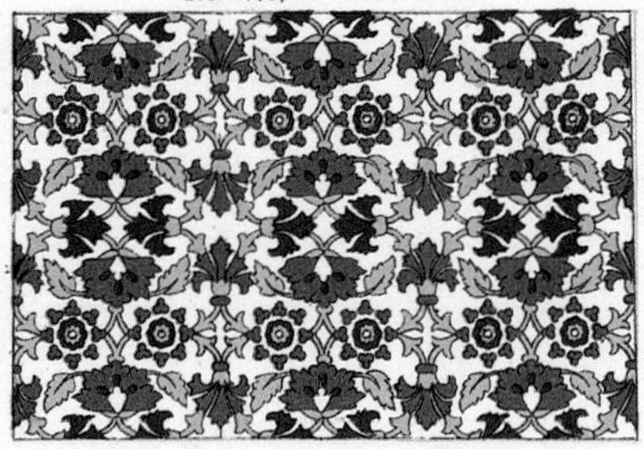

No. 1191-2-3-4, P. 6in. Tiles.

No. 1185, P. 6in. Tiles.

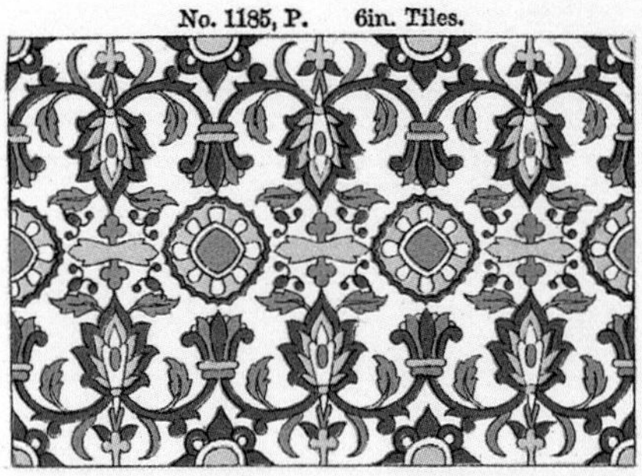

o. 2, P.

6in. Tiles.

No. 1176. P.

6in. Tiles.

No. 1178, P. 6in. Tiles.

No. 1175, P. 6in. Tiles.

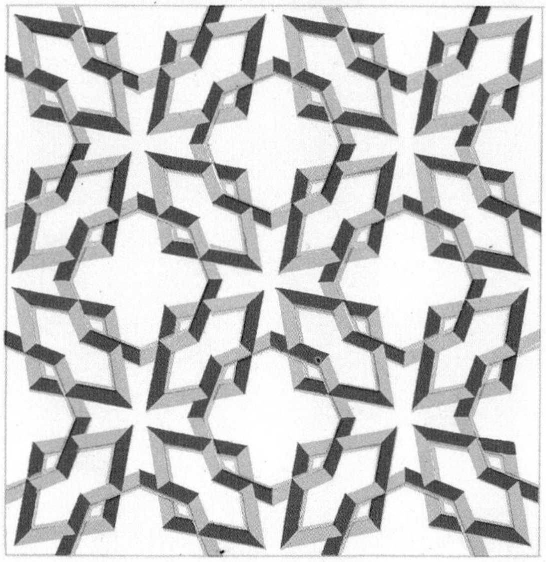

No. 1187, P. 6in. Tiles.

8in. × 4in. Tiles.

8in. × 8in. Tiles.

No. 1234, P. 8in. Tiles.

No. 1233, P. 8in. Tiles.

Postal Address,—
MINTONS, (LIMITED)—
CHINA WORKS,
STOKE-UPON-TRENT.

Scale 1 2 3 4 5 6 7 8 9 10 11 12 1½ *In to a foot.*
INCHES.

T. Forman and Sons, Nottingham.

MINTONS, (LIMITED)—CHINA WORKS: STOKE-UPON-TRENT, AND 28, WALBROOK, LONDON.

TILES RICHLY GLAZED AND DECORATED WITH ENAMELS

FOR FIRE-PLACES, HEARTHS, FURNITURE, FRIEZES, WALLS, AND OTHER ARCHITECTURAL DECORATION, FLOWER-BOXES, &c.

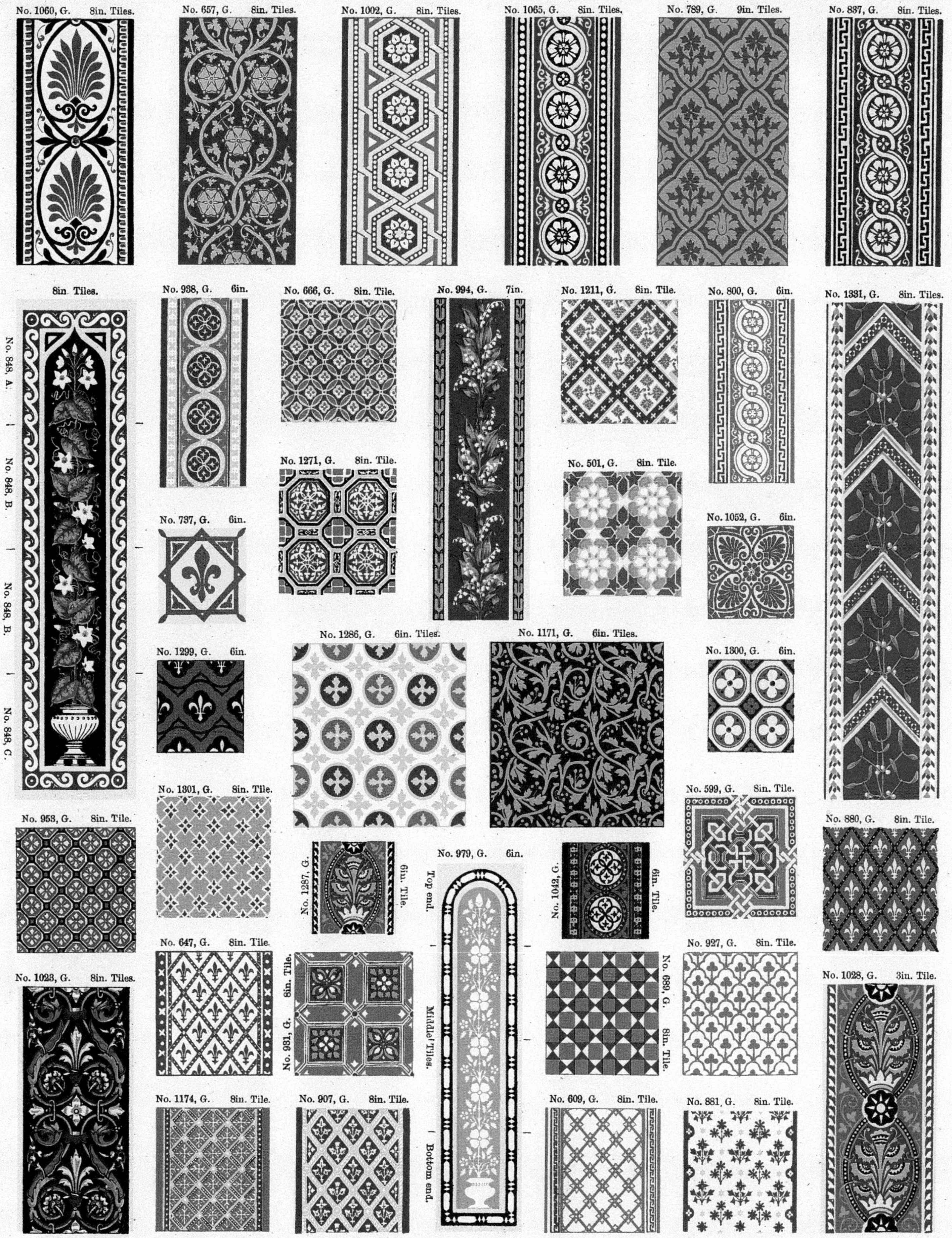

Postal Address,—
MINTONS, (LIMITED)—
CHINA WORKS,
STOKE-UPON-TRENT.

Scale 1 2 3 4 5 6 7 8 9 10 11 12 *1½ In. to a foot.*
INCHES

N.B.—Nos. 953, 647, 880, 666, 927, 907, 881, and 689 are also made in 6in. Tiles; and Nos. 1052, and 1171, as 8in. Tiles.

T. Forman and Sons, Nottingham.

MINTONS, (LIMITED)—CHINA WORKS: STOKE-UPON-TRENT, AND 28, WALBROOK, LONDON.

TILES RICHLY GLAZED AND DECORATED WITH ENAMELS

FOR WALLS, FRIEZES, AND OTHER ARCHITECTURAL DECORATION, FURNITURE, FIRE-PLACES, HEARTHS, FLOWER-BOXES, &c.

No. 43, G. 8in. Tiles.

No. 650, G. 8in. × 4in. Tiles.

No. 991, G. 8in. Tiles.

No. 1167, G. 8in. × 4in. Tiles.

No. 602, G. 8in. Tiles.

No. 756, G. 6in. × 3in. Tiles.

No. 1036, G. 6in. Tiles.

No. 855, G. 6in. Tiles.

No. 853, G. 6in. Tiles.

No. 1037, G. No. 1040, G. 6in. Tiles. No. 1039, G. No. 1038, G.

No. 839, G. 6in. × 3in. Tiles.

No. 902, G. 6in. Tiles.

No. 796, G. 6in. Tiles.

No. 577, G. 6in. Tiles.

No. 1044, G. 6in. Tiles.

No. 834, G. 6in. × 3in. Tiles.

No. 753, G. 6in. × 3in. Tiles.

No. 603, G. 6in. Tiles.

No. 740, G. 6in. Tiles.

No. 794, G. 6in. Tiles.

No. 611, G. 6in. Tiles.

No. 842, A. n. × 2in.

No. 545, G. 3in Tiles.

No. 1260, G. 3in. × 6in.

No. 765, G. 6in. Tiles.

No. 742, G. 6in. × 3in.

No. 826, G. 6in. Tiles.

Postal Address,—
MINTONS, (LIMITED)—
CHINA WORKS,
STOKE-UPON-TRENT.

Scale 1 2 3 4 5 6 7 8 9 10 11 12 *1½ In. to a foot.* INCHES

N.B.—No. 602, G. is also made in 6in. and 7in. Tiles; and No. 1044, in 8in Tiles.

T. Forman and Sons, Nottingham.

MINTONS:—CHINA WORKS: STOKE-UPON-TRENT, AND 28, WALBROOK, LONDON.

TILES RICHLY GLAZED AND DECORATED WITH ENAMELS

FOR FLOWER-BOXES, FRIEZES, WALLS, AND OTHER ARCHITECTURAL DECORATION, FURNITURE, HEARTHS, FIRE-PLACES, &c.

No. 489, G 8in. Tiles.

No. 792, G. 7in. Tiles.

No. 985, G. 8in. Tiles.

No. 965, G. 6in. Tiles.

No. 566, G. 8in. Tiles.

No. 1027, G. 6in. Tiles.

No. 949, G. 8in. Tiles.

No. 968, G. 6in. Tiles.

No. 813, G. 6in. × 3in. Tiles.

No. 969. G. 6in × 3in. Tiles.

No. 764, G. 6in. Tiles.

No. 1288, G. 6in. Tiles.

No. 498, G. 8in. Tiles.

No. 797, G. 6in. Tiles.

No. 827, G. 6in. Tiles.

No. 499, G. 6in. Tiles.

No. 963, G. 6in. Tiles.

Postal Address,—
MINTONS:—
CHINA WORKS,
STOKE-UPON-TRENT.

Scale INCHES *1½ In. to a foot*

N.B.—No 797, G. is also made as an 8in. Tile, and No. 949, G. as a 6in. Tile.

T. Forman and Sons, Nottingham.

MINTONS, (LIMITED)—CHINA WORKS: STOKE-UPON-TRENT, AND 28, WALBROOK, LONDON.

TILES RICHLY GLAZED AND DECORATED WITH ENAMELS

FOR FLOWER-BOXES, FRIEZES, WALLS AND OTHER ARCHITECTURAL DECORATION, FURNITURE, HEARTHS, FIRE-PLACES, &c

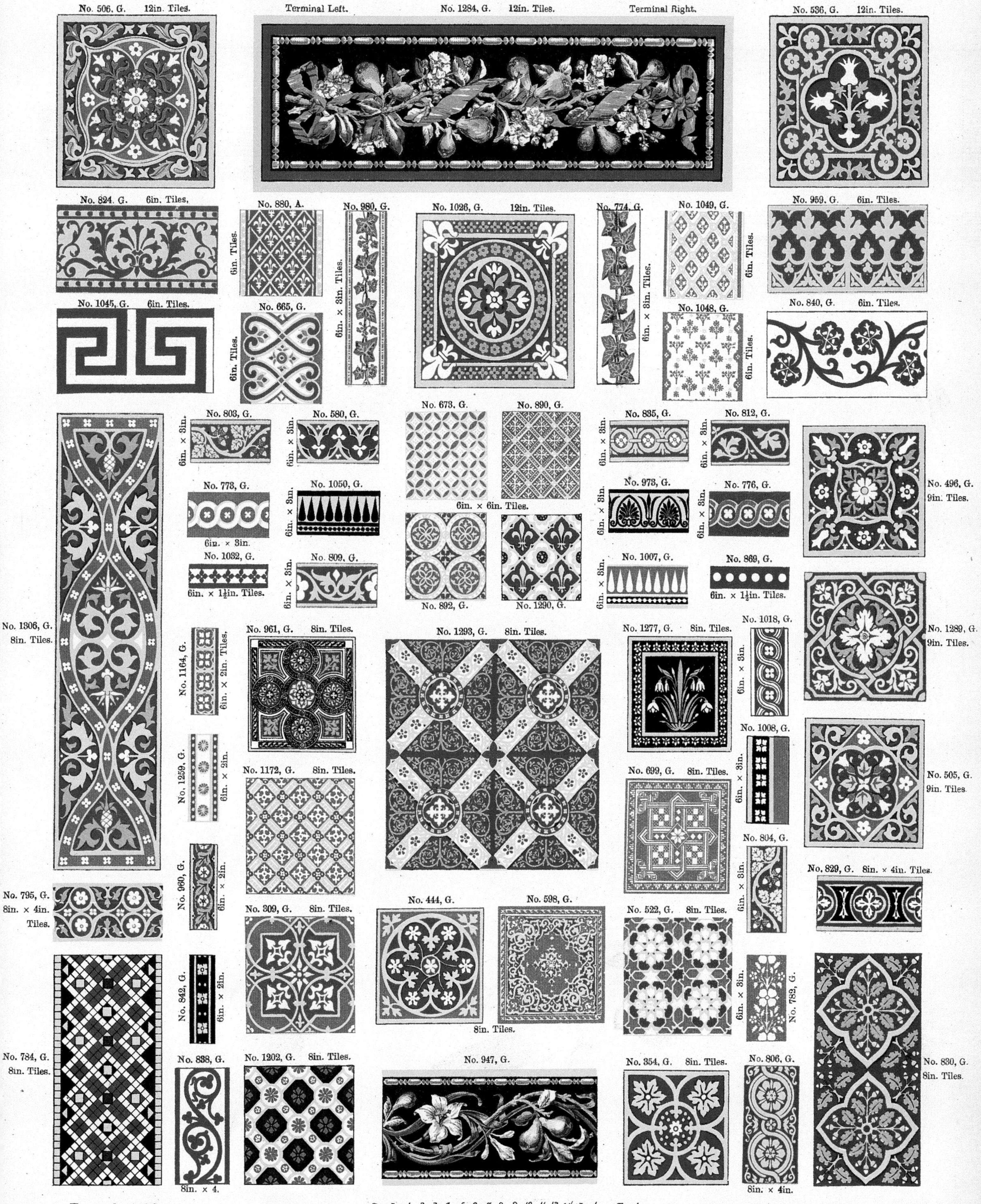

Scale 1 2 3 4 5 6 7 8 9 10 11 12 *1½ In to a Foot*
INCHES.

N.B.—Nos. 880, A, 665, 1049, 1048, and 673 are also made in 8in. Tiles; and Nos. 1277 and 830 in 6in. Tiles.

Postal Address,—
MINTONS, (LIMITED)—
CHINA WORKS,
STOKE-UPON-TRENT.

T. Forman and Sons, Nottingham.

MINTONS:—CHINA WORKS: STOKE-UPON-TRENT, AND 28, WALBROOK, LONDON.

TILES RICHLY GLAZED AND DECORATED IN GOLD, SILVER, AND ENAMELS.

FOR FIRE-PLACES, HEARTHS, FURNITURE, JARDINIERES, FRIEZES, AND OTHER ARCHITECTURAL DECORATION, &c.

No. 1445 P. 6in. Tiles.

No. 1390 P. 8in. Tiles.

No. 1421 P. 8in. Tiles.

No. 1399 P. 6in. Tiles

No. 1402 P. 8in. Tiles.

Bottom END Tile.

No. 1446 P. 6in. Tiles.

No. 1392 P. 8in. Tiles.

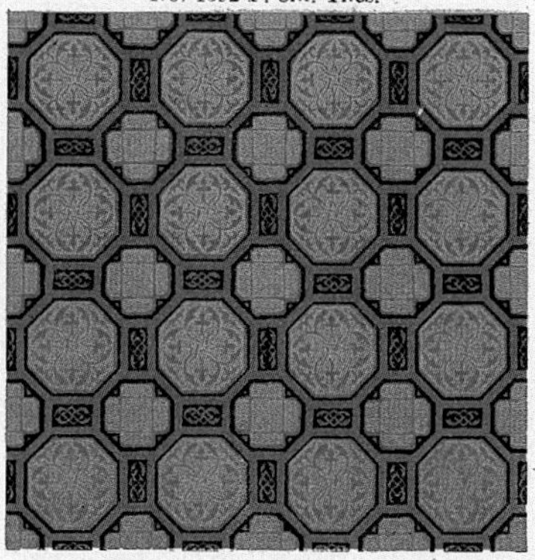

No. 1388. P. 8in. Tiles.

No. 1443 P. 6in. Tiles.

N.B.—THE ABOVE PATTERNS ARE ON A BRILLIANT PERSIAN TORQUOISE GLAZE, WHICH IS ONLY IMPERFECTLY REPRESENTED IN THIS PRINT. THESE ARE NOT SUITABLE FOR HEARTHS.

No. 1448. G. 6in. Tiles.

No. 1450 G. 6in. Tiles.

No. 1444 G. 6in. Tiles.

No. 1451 G. 6in. Tiles.

No. 1447 G. 6in. Tiles.

No. 1426 G. 8in. Tiles.

Bottom END Tile.

No. 1452 G. 8in. Tiles.

No. 1449 G. 6in. Tiles.

No. 1453 G 8in. Tiles.

No. 1427 G. 8in. Tiles.

END Tile.

J. FLEMING & CO., LITH., LEICESTER.

Scale 1 2 3 4 5 6 7 8 9 10 11 12 *1½ In, to a foot.* INCHES

Postal Address,
MINTONS:—
CHINA WORKS,
STOKE-UPON-TRENT.

N.B.— No. 1390 is also made as a 6in. Tile, and No. 1446, as an 8in. In the patterns with gold and color, on white ground, the Color may be varied.

MINTONS (LIMITED)—CHINA WORKS: STOKE-UPON-TRENT, AND 28, WALBROOK, LONDON.

TILES RICHLY GLAZED AND DECORATED IN GOLD, SILVER, AND ENAMELS,

FOR FIRE-PLACES, HEARTHS, FURNITURE, JARDINIERES, FRIEZES, AND OTHER ARCHITECTURAL DECORATION, &c.

No. 1413. G. 6in. Tiles.

No. 1386. G. 8in. Tiles.

No. 1412. G. 6in. Tiles.

No. 1418. G. 6in.

No. 1441. G. 8in. Tiles.

No. 1417. G. 6in.

No. 1376. G. 6in. Tiles.

No. 1435. G. 6in.

No. 1436. G. 6in.

No. 1374. G. 6in. Tiles.

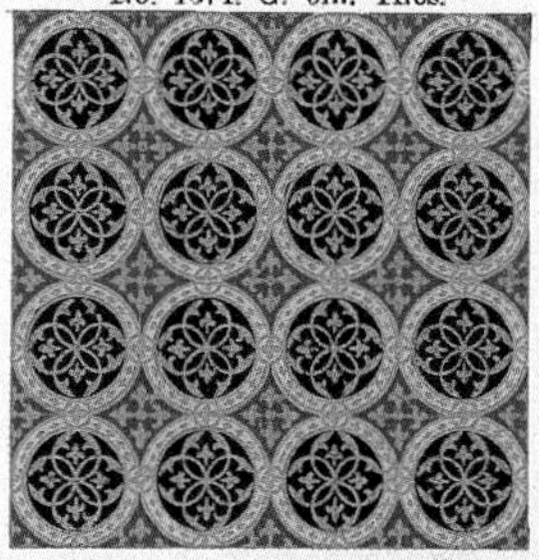

No. 1437. G. 8in. Tiles.

Bottom END Tile.

No. 1369. G. 4in. Tiles.

No. 1438. G. 6in. Tile.

No. 1370. G. 6in. Tiles.

No. 1372. G. 6in. Tiles.

No. 1420. G. 8in. Tiles.

END Tile.

No. 1442. G. 8in. Tiles.

No. 1439. G. 8in. Tiles.

No. 1373. G. 6in. Tiles.

No. 1375. G. 6in. Tiles.

No. 1387. G. 6in.

No. 1414. G. 8in. Tiles.

No. 1440. 6in.

J. FLEMING & CO., LITH., LEICESTER.

Scale. 1 2 3 4 5 6 7 8 9 10 11 12 *1½ In. to a foot.*
INCHES.

Postal Address,—
MINTONS (LIMITED):—
CHINA WORKS,
STOKE-UPON-TRENT.

N.B.—Patterns Nos. 1435 and 1440 are also made in 8in. Tiles, and No. 1442 in 6in.

MINTONS (LIMITED)—CHINA WORKS: STOKE-UPON-TRENT, AND 28, WALBROOK, LONDON.

GLAZED TILES WITH ORDINARY PRINTED PATTERNS.

These are all done on the usual ⅜" thick Tiles and the 6" × 6" are also done on extra-thick Tiles for Hearths, &c., when these last are wanted, an X should be added to the No.

No. 1506. G. 8" Tiles. No. 1507. G.

No. 1562. G. 8" Tiles.

No. 1682. G. 8" Tiles.

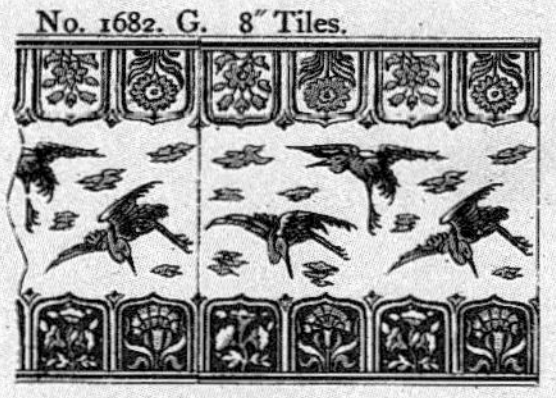

No. 1509. G. 8" Tiles. No. 1508. G.

No. 1561. G. 8" Tiles.

No. 1505. G. 8" Tiles.

Nos. 1503 & 4. G. 8"

No. 1560. G. 8" Tiles.

No. 1320. G. 8" Tiles.

No. 1811. G. 8" Tiles.

No. 54. G. 6" Tiles.

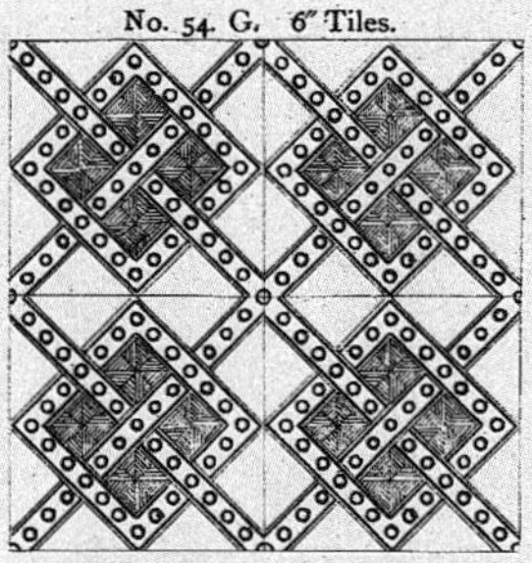

Marble. 6" Tiles.

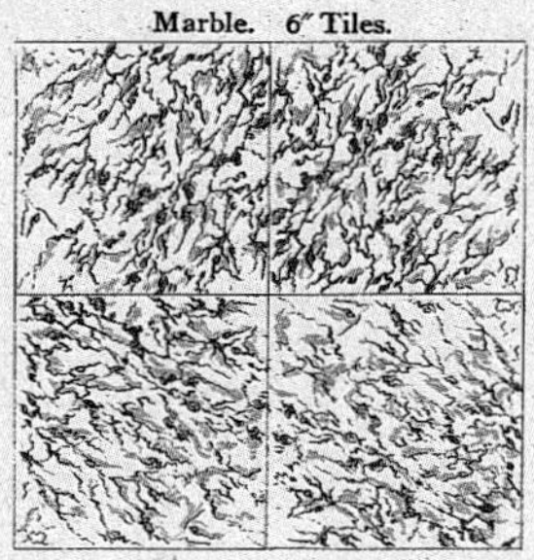

No. 1801. G. 6"

12 Subjects.

No. 1699. G. 6"

12 Subjects.

No. 1643. G. 6" Tiles.

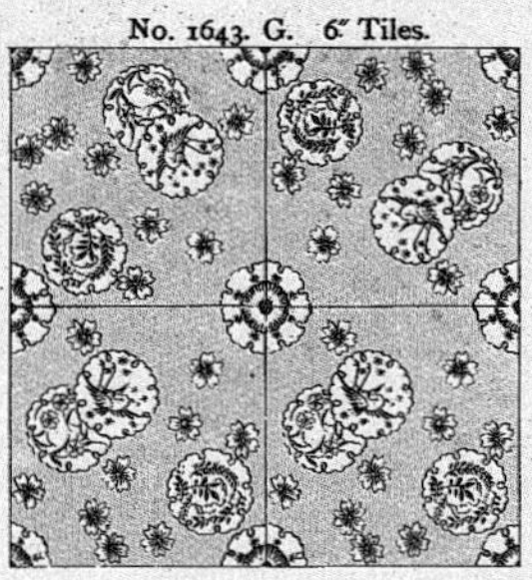

No. 1783. G. 6" Tiles.

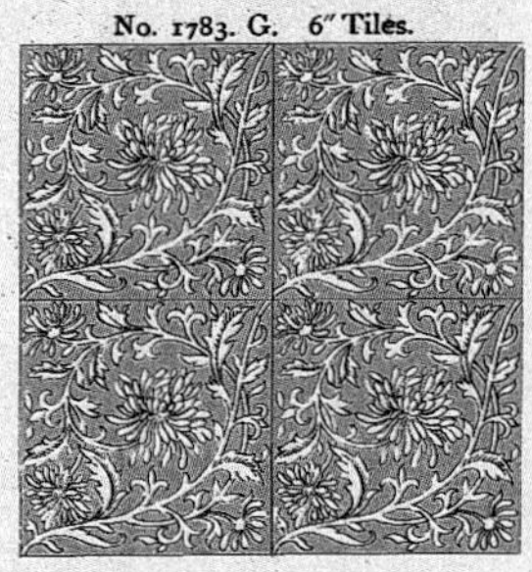

No. 1540. G. 6" Tiles.

No. 1538. G. 6" Tiles.

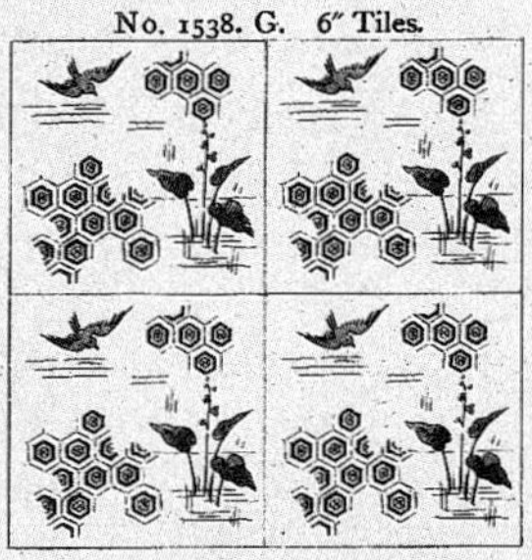

No. 12. G. 6"

12 Subjects.

No. 57. G. 6"

8 Subjects.

No. 1537. G. 6" Tiles.

No. 1536. G. 6" Tiles.

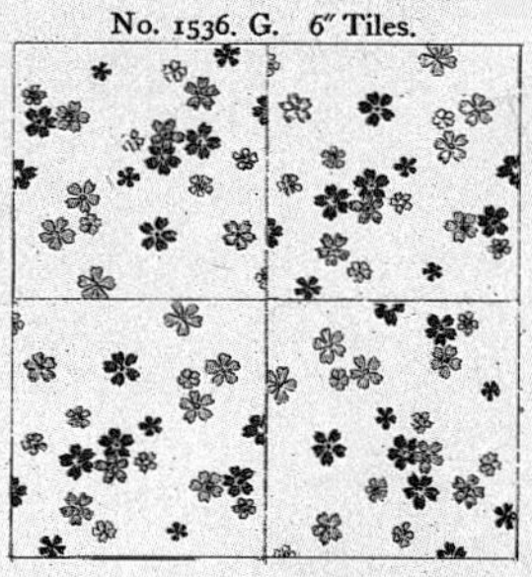

No. 1645. G. 6 × 3"

No. 1822. G. 6 × 3"

No. 1784. G. 6"

No. 1760. G. 6"

No. 58. G. 6"

4 Subjects.

No. 1541. G. 6"

No. 36 G. 6"

12 Subjects.

No. 1807. G. 6"

No. 1808. G. 6"

No. 1567. G. 6"

6 × 3" Top.

6 × 6" Centre Tiles.

6 × 3" Bottom.

No. 1539. G. 6"

No. 27. G. 6" Tiles.

B A

C D

No. 1706. G. 6" Tiles.

No. 1741. G. 6" Tiles.

The colour here represented is Indian Blue on White Tiles, but the same patterns are also done in Black, in Deep Brown, and in a rather clearer Blue called F. Blue. They are also done on Ivory and Buff Tiles.

Postal Address,—
MINTONS (LIMITED):—
CHINA WORKS,
STOKE-UPON-TRENT.

Scale 1 2 3 4 5 6 7 8 9 10 11 12 *1½ In. to a foot*
INCHES.

J. Fleming & Co. Lith., Leicester.

N. B.—No. 1643 is also made 8". Nos. 1537 & 1538 are somtimes used alternately. The End Tile of No. 1811 may be 8" × 4".

MINTONS:—CHINA WORKS: STOKE-UPON-TRENT, AND 28, WALBROOK, LONDON.

TILES RICHLY GLAZED AND DECORATED WITH ENAMELS,

FOR FIRE-PLACES, HEARTHS, FURNITURE, FRIEZES, WALLS, AND OTHER ARCHITECTURAL DECORATION, FLOWER-BOXES, &c.

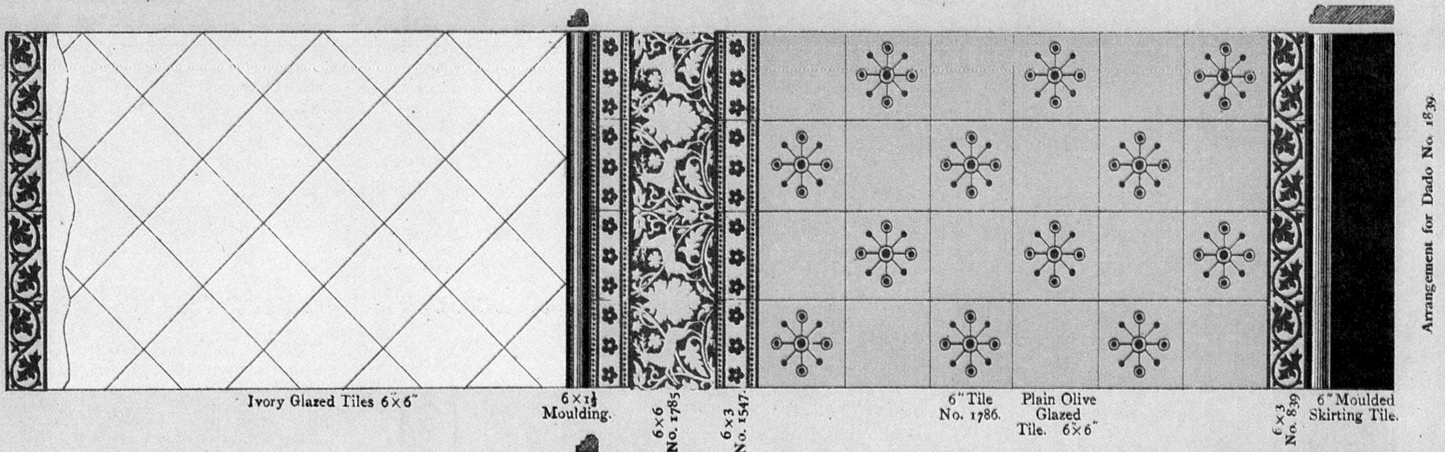

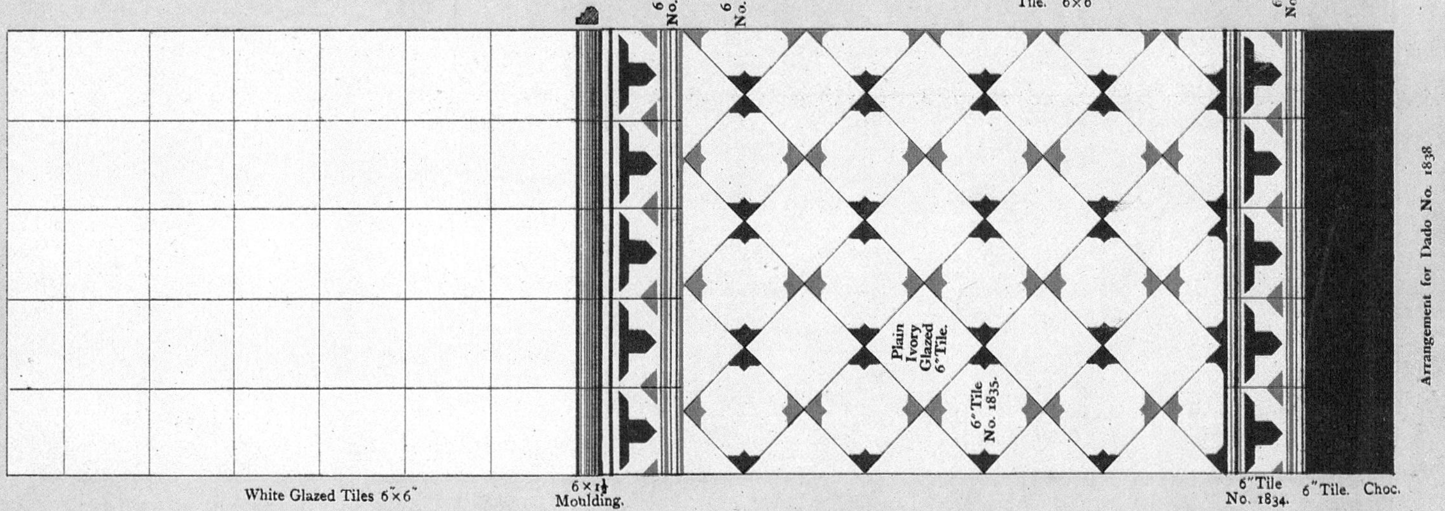

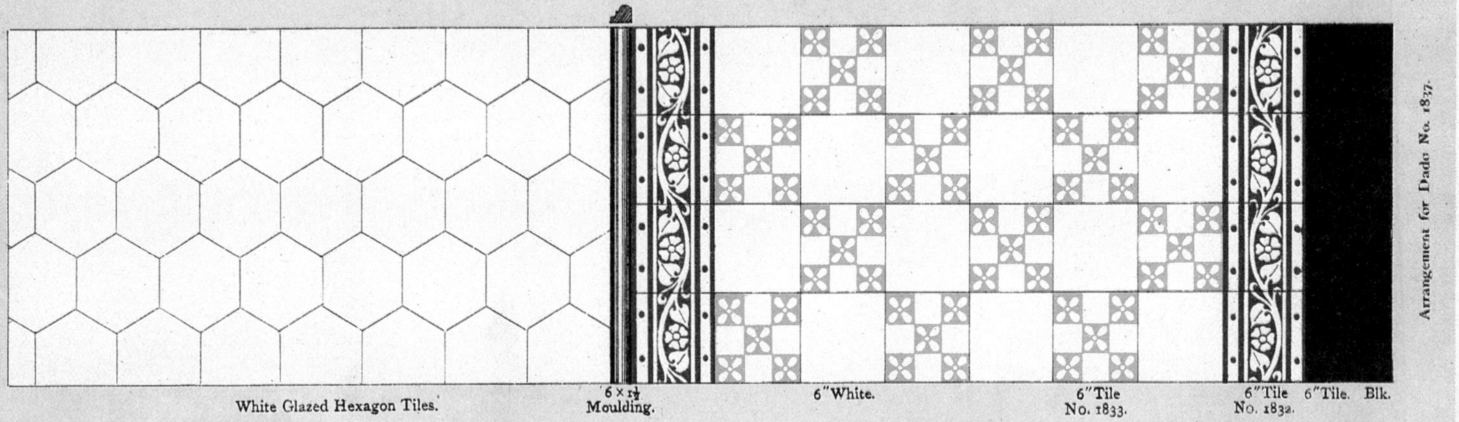

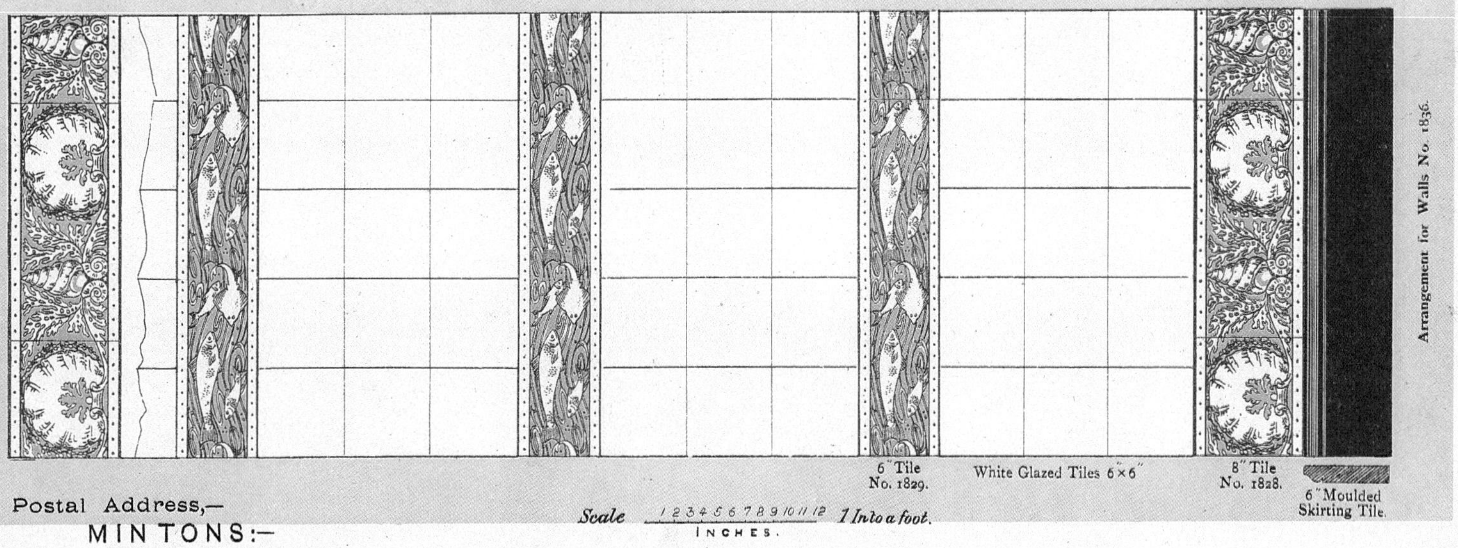

Postal Address,—
MINTONS:—
CHINA WORKS,
STOKE-UPON-TRENT

Scale 1 2 3 4 5 6 7 8 9 10 11 12 INCHES. *1 In to a foot.*

J. Fleming & Co., Lith., Leicester.

MINTONS (LIMITED)—CHINA WORKS: STOKE-UPON-TRENT, AND 28, WALBROOK, LONDON.

TILES RICHLY GLAZED AND DECORATED WITH ENAMELS.

Suitable patterns are done both on the Extra Thick body for HEARTHS, and on the Ordinary body for Walls, &c. The purpose should be stated when ordering.

N. B.—Nos. 1717 and 1718 are also made in 8in. Tiles. In the Single Colour patterns the No. does not always express the Colour or the Body, these may be varied and should be given when ordering. The NAMES of the colours and bodies are given above.

Postal Address,—
MINTONS (LIMITED):—
CHINA WORKS,
STOKE-UPON-TRENT.

Scale .... 1½ In. to a foot.
INCHES

J. Fleming & Co. Lith., Leicester

MINTONS (LIMITED)—CHINA WORKS: STOKE-UPON-TRENT, AND 28, WALBROOK, LONDON.

TILES RICHLY GLAZED AND DECORATED WITH ENAMELS.

Suitable patterns are done both on the Extra Thick body for HEARTHS, and on the Ordinary body for Walls, &c The purpose should be stated when ordering.

J. Fleming & Co. Lith., Leicester

Postal Address,—
MINTONS (LIMITED):—
CHINA WORKS,
STOKE-UPON-TRENT.

Scale. 1 2 3 4 5 6 7 8 9 10 11 12 *1½ In. to a foot.* INCHES.

N.B.—Patterns similar to Nos. 1821 and 1840 are done on 6in. tiles.

MINTONS (LIMITED)—CHINA WORKS: STOKE-UPON-TRENT, AND 28, WALBROOK, LONDON.

TILES RICHLY GLAZED AND DECORATED WITH ENAMELS.

Suitable patterns are done both on the Extra Thick body for HEARTHS, and on the Ordinary body for Walls, &c. The purpose should be stated when ordering.

No. 1794. G. 6in. Tiles.

Border 6×3. No. 1823. G.

No. 1700. G. 6in. Tiles.

Border 6×3. No. 1725. G.

No. 1698. G. 8in. Tiles.

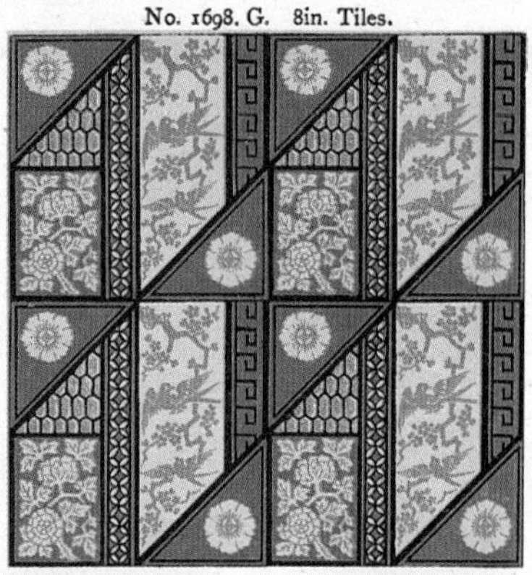

No. 1703. G. 6in. Tiles.

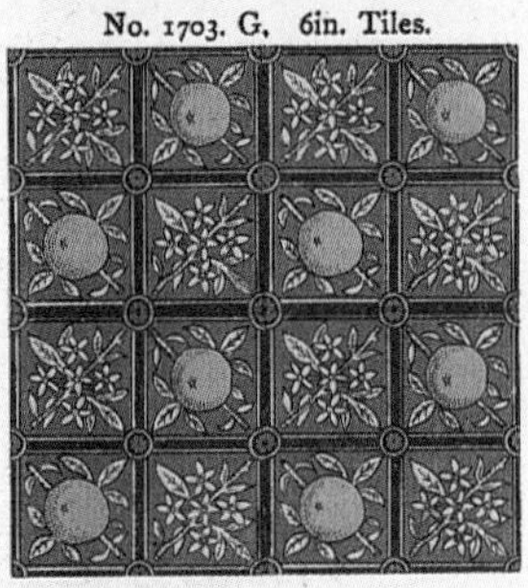

No. 1677 G. 6in. Tiles.

Tennyson's Idylls. 12 subjects.
In Sepia Monochrome.

No. 1843. G. Sepia Monochrome. 6in.

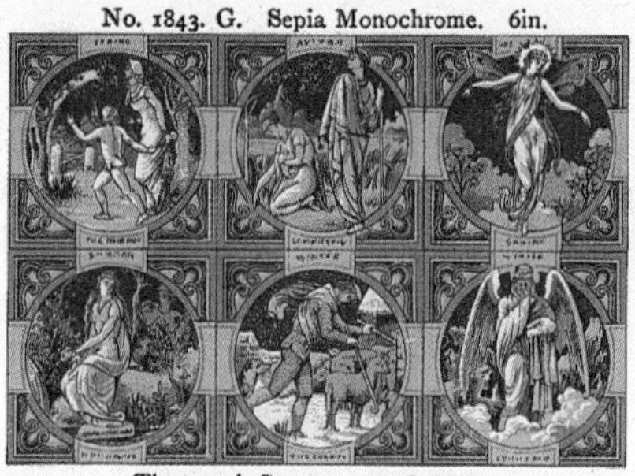

Thomson's Seasons. 12 Subjects
4 of them Emblematical.

No. 1844. Grey Mono.

No. 1773. 6×1¼.

Thomson's Seasons.

No. 1868. G.

Grey. Sepia. Waverley Series in 6in. Tiles.

No. 1686. G. 8in. Tiles.

Top Terminal. Middle Tiles. Bottom Terminal.

No. 1862. G. 8in. Tiles.

No. 1704. G. 6in.

Top End. Middle Tiles. Bottom End.

No. 1705. G. 6in.

No. 1778. G. 6in. Tiles.

No. 1779. G. 6in. Tiles.

No. 1684. 6×1¼.

No. 1773. 6×1¼.

Grey Monochrome. 18 Subjects. 6in.

No. 1665. Shakespeare.

No. 1685. 6×1.

No. 1772. G. 8×2.

Sepia Monochrome.

No. 1710. Skapespeare. 8in.
18 Subjects.

No. 1771. G. 8×2.

Grey Monochrome.

No. 1607. Waverley.
12 Subjects.

Top End.

Middle Tile. No. 1696. G. Sepia Monoe. No. 1709. G.

Bottom End.

8×4 Top.

No. 1714. G. 8in.

No. 1697. G. Waverley Sepia Monoe.

8×4 Bottom.

No. 1711. G. 6in. Tiles.

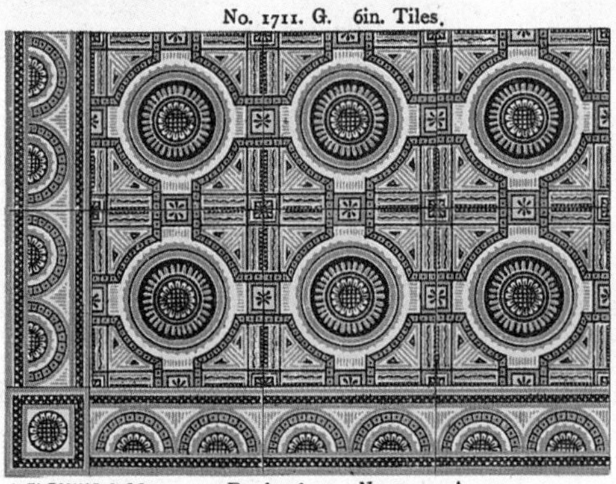

J. FLEMING & CO., Border 6×3. No. 1730. A.

No. 1708. G. 6in. Tiles.

Border 6×3. No. 1764. A.

No. 1723. G. 6in. Tiles.

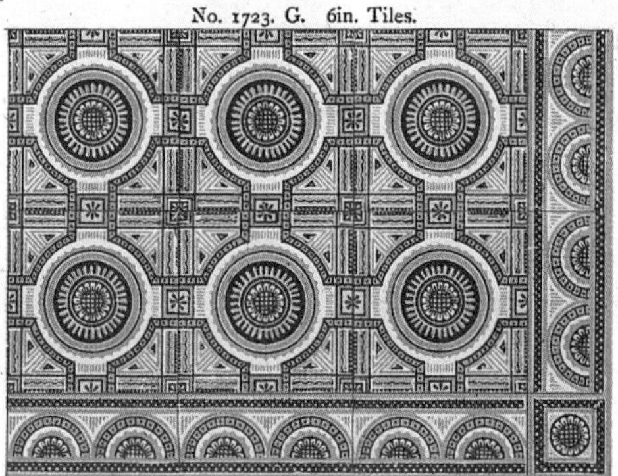

Border 6×3. No. 1730. B. LITH.: LEICESTER.

Postal Address,—
MINTONS (LIMITED):—
CHINA WORKS,
STOKE-UPON-TRENT.

Scale. 1 2 3 4 5 6 7 8 9 10 11 12 *1½ In. to a foot*
INCHES.

N.B.—The Terminal Tile in Nos. 1686, 1862 and 1714 may be either 8×4 or 8×8.

MINTONS (LIMITED)—CHINA WORKS: STOKE-UPON-TRENT, AND 28, WALBROOK, LONDON.

TILES RICHLY GLAZED AND DECORATED WITH ENAMELS.

Suitable patterns are done both on the Extra Thick body for HEARTHS, and on the Ordinary body for Walls, &c. The purpose should be stated when ordering.

No. 1852. G.

panel 32× 8 for Left Side.

No. 1854. G.

This pattern is also arranged for running horizontally.

panel 30× 6 or 36× 6.

No. 1733. G.

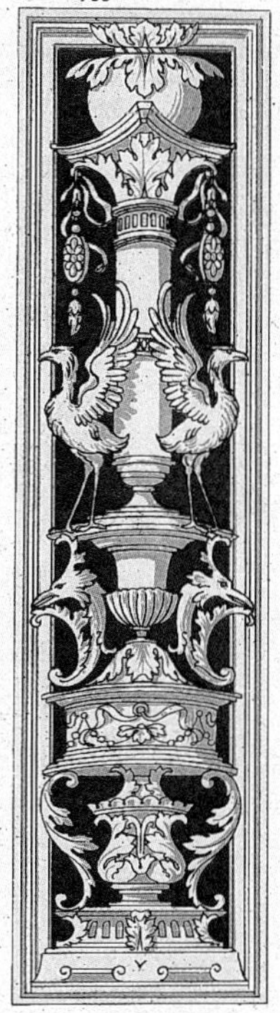

panel 32× 8.

No. 1815. Green Gd.

panel 32× 8.

No. 1855. G.

This pattern is also arranged for running horizontally.

panel 30×6 or 36×6.

No. 1853. G.

panel 32×8 for Right Side.

No. 1873. G.

panel 30×6 or 36×6.

No. 1546. G.

Tiles 6×6.

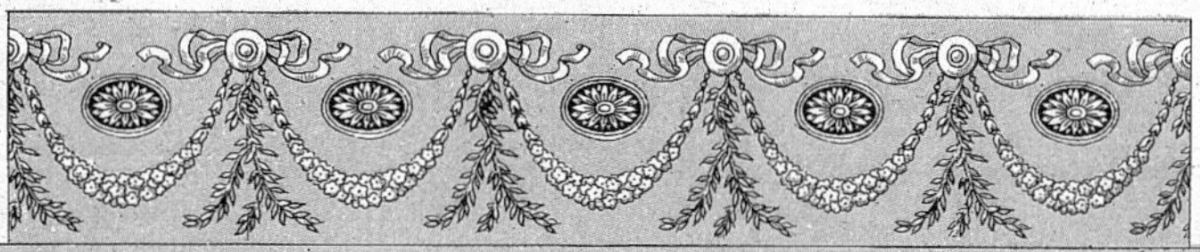

No. 1739. G. Hearth, Queen Anne Style.

No. 1861. G.

Tile 6×6.

No. 1841. G.

Top terminal.

Middle tiles.

Bottom terminal.

Tiles 6×6.

No. 1866. G. 6in. Tiles.

Border 6×3. No. 1858. G.

No. 1856. G.

Border No. 1858. G.

This pattern, Nos. 1866 & 1856, look well placed alternately.

No. 1815. Choc. Gd.

panels 32×8.

No. 1827. G.

No. 1859. G. 6in. Tiles.

Border 6×3. No. 1860. G.

No. 1781. G. 6in. Tiles.

Border 6×3 No. 1782. G.

J. FLEMING & CO., LITH., LEICESTER.

Postal Address,—
MINTONS (LIMITED):—
CHINA WORKS,
STOKE-UPON-TRENT.

Scale 1 2 3 4 5 6 7 8 9 10 11 12 *1½ In. to a foot*
INCHES

N. B.—The 6″ pattern No. 1873 may also be done in the same Colours as the 8″ pattern. Nos. 1815 and 1827 and the 8″ in the same as the 6″. No. 1841 may also be done in Colours as Nos. 1456 and 1457 sheet 2.

MINTONS (LIMITED)—CHINA WORKS: STOKE-UPON-TRENT, AND 28, WALBROOK, LONDON.

TILES RICHLY GLAZED AND DECORATED WITH ENAMELS.

The patterns on this sheet are specially designed for HEARTHS, for which an extra thick body is used, but they are also done on ordinary Tiles for Grates, Walls, &c. The purpose should be stated in ordering.

No. 1933. G. 6in. Tiles.

6 x 3in. Border. No. 1985. G.

No. 1975. G. 6in. Tiles.

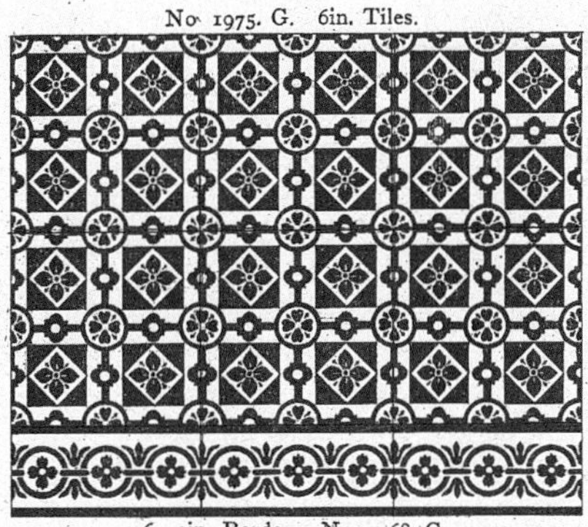

6 x 3in. Border. No. 1268. G.
Chocolate on White body.

No. 1931. G. 6in. Tiles.

6 x 3in. Border. No. 1725. G.

No. 1929. G. 6in. Tiles.

Chocolate on Buff body.

No. 1936. G. 6in. Tiles. No. 1938. G.

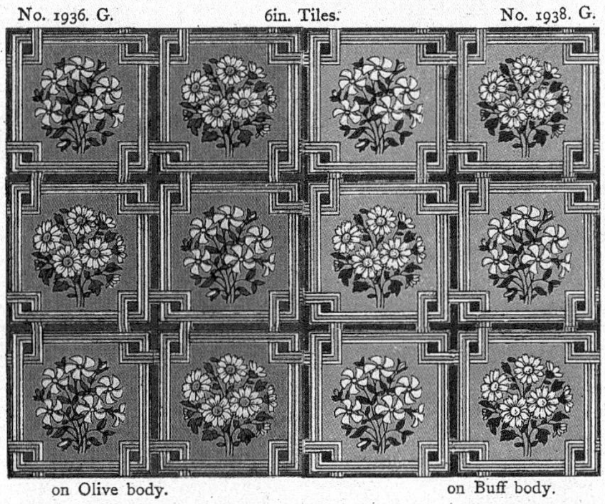

on Olive body. on Buff body.

No. 1989. G. 6in. Tiles.

Black on White body.

No. 1904. G. 6in. Tiles

6 x 3in. Border. No. 1905. G.

No. 1948. G. 6in. Tiles.

6 x 3in. Border. No. 1986. G.

No. 1889. G. 6in. Tiles.

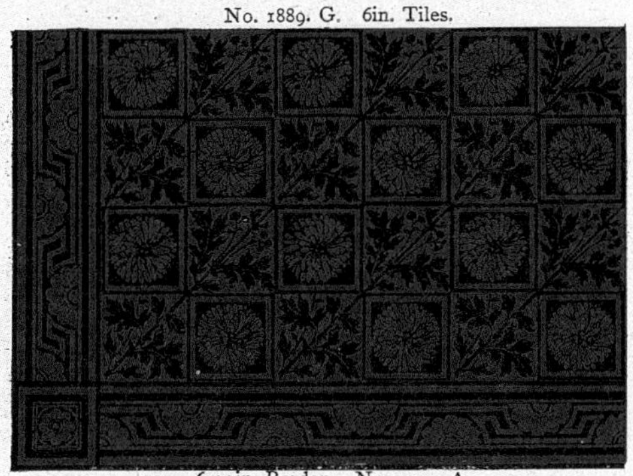

6 x 3in. Border. No. 1744. A.
Black on Red body.

No. 1916. G. 6in. Tiles.

6 x 3in. Border. No. 803. A.
Chocolate on Buff body.

No. 1974. G. 6in. Tiles.

6 x 3in. Border. No. 1988. G.
Black on Drab body.

J. FLEMING & CO., LITH., LEICESTER.

Postal Address,—
MINTONS (LIMITED):—
CHINA WORKS,
STOKE-UPON-TRENT.

Scale 1 2 3 4 5 6 7 8 9 10 11 12 *1½ In. to a foot*
INCHES.

N.B.—The patterns in One Colour may be varied both in the Tint of the Body and Colour of the Pattern:—thus Black on White may be substituted for Chocolate on Buff, &c. There are also other Colourings of some of the richer patterns.

MINTONS:—CHINA WORKS: STOKE-UPON-TRENT, AND 28, WALBROOK, LONDON.

TILES RICHLY GLAZED AND DECORATED WITH ENAMELS.

Suitable patterns are done both on the Extra Thick body for HEARTHS, and on the Ordinary body for Walls, &c. The purpose should be stated when ordering.

No. 1960. G.

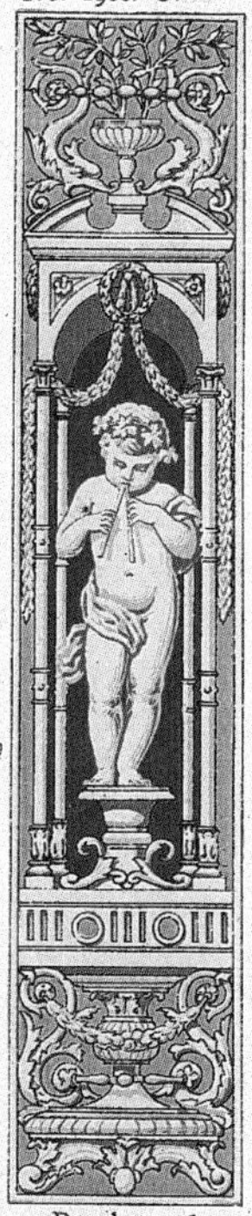

Figure for Left Side.

Panel 30 × 6.

Arrangement. No. 1970:—Frieze for Side Panels No. 1960. G

This Frieze may also be done in same Colors as the Side Panel No. 1999. G.

No. 1999. G.

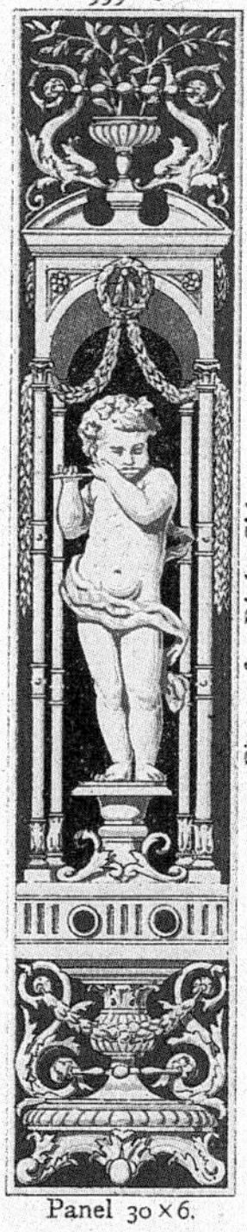

Figure for Right Side.

Panel 30 × 6.

No. 1944 G. No. 1941. G.

6in. Tiles.

No. 1907. G. 8in. Tile.

Made also in 6in.

No. 1997. G. No. 1993. G.

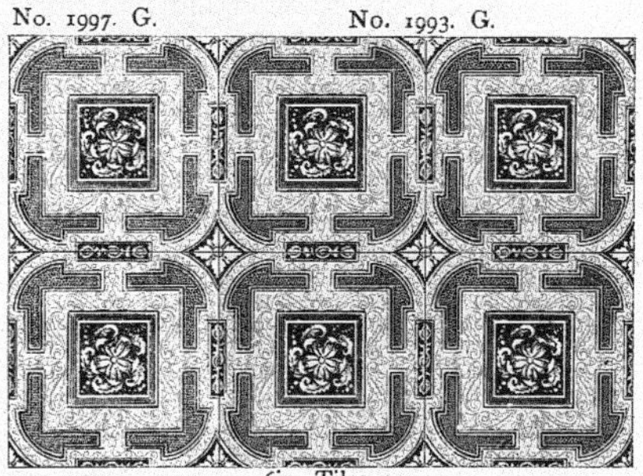

6in. Tiles.

No. 1908. G. 8in.

Made also in 6in.

No. 1925. G. No. 1901. G.

6in. Tiles.

No. 1969. G. No. 1981. G.

The Side Tiles may be done in these Colors.

No. 1909 G. 8in.

Made also in 6in.

No. 1955. G.

Top End Tile. Middle Tiles. Bottom End Tile.

8in. Tiles.

No. 1971. G.

Top End Tile. Middle Tiles. Bottom End Tile.

No. 1992. G.

No. 1939. G. 6in Tiles.

No. 1940. G. 6in. Tiles.

No. 1968. G.

6in. Tiles.

No. 1976. G.

No. 1978. G.

The Hearth Tiles may be done in these Colors.

No 1942 G. 6in. Tiles.

No. 1998. G. 6in. Tiles.

No. 1886. G. 6in. Tiles.

Deep Brown on Buff.

No. 1915. G. 6in. Tiles.

Deep Brown on White.

No. 1892. G. 6in. Tiles.

India Blue on White.

No. 1911-12. G. 6in. Tiles.

Deep Brown on White.

No. 1887. G. 6in. Tiles.

Deep Brown on Ivory.

Any of the patterns in this lower row may be done in Black, Deep Brown, India Blue or Green, on White Tiles, and also on Buff or Ivory Tiles. See similar patterns on Sheet 16.

Postal Address,—
MINTONS:—
CHINA WORKS,
STOKE-UPON-TRENT

Scale 1 2 3 4 5 6 7 8 9 10 11 12 1½ In. to a foot
INCHES.

J. Fleming & Co. Lith., Leicester

MINTONS (LIMITED)—CHINA WORKS: STOKE-UPON-TRENT, AND 28, WALBROOK, LONDON.

TILES RICHLY GLAZED AND DECORATED WITH ENAMELS.

The patterns on this sheet are specially designed for HEARTHS, for which an extra thick body is used, but they are also done on ordinary Tiles for Grates, Walls, &c. The purpose should be stated in ordering.

No. 2002. A. No. 2002. B.

The 6 × 6 tiles No. 2002. A. & B. The 6 × 3 border No. 2003.

No. 2000.

The 6 × 6 tiles No. 2000 The 6 × 3 border No. 2001.

POMPEIAN MOSAIC HEARTH. No. 1995.

No. 2008.

The 6×6 tiles No. 2008. The 6×3 border 2003.

No. 2009.

The 6×6 tiles No. 2009. The 6×3 border No. 2012.

Postal Address,—
MINTONS (LIMITED):—
CHINA WORKS,
STOKE-UPON-TRENT.

Scale 1 2 3 4 5 6 7 8 9 10 11 12 1½ In. to a foot
INCHES.

J. Fleming & Co. Lith., Leicester